Damnyankee

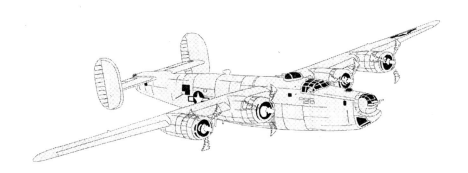

US Navy PB4Y-1 Liberator

Thomas L. Walsh

Tony Walsh

August, 2009

Damnyankee

A WWII Story of Tragedy and Survival
off the West of Ireland

Outskirts Press, Inc.
Denver, Colorado

Outskirts Press, Inc.
http://www.outskirtspress.com

ISBN: 978-1-4327-2910-3

Library of Congress Control Number: 2008936961

Outskirts Press and the "OP" logo are trademarks belonging to Outskirts Press, Inc.

PRINTED IN THE UNITED STATES OF AMERICA

This book is dedicated to my friend,
James O. Trudeau

"In all our reasonings concerning men
We must lay it down as a maxim
That the greater parts are moulded
By circumstances."

--Robert Hall

CONTENTS

ACKNOWLEDGEMENTS

Anyone who has ever undertaken writing a book understands the self-doubt, nervousness and occasional despair I've experienced over the past several years.

Special thanks to Deb Barracato and my dear wife Wynne Ann Walsh, who were both amongst the earliest to tell me yes, I could do this.

Of course, Sean Kelly and Jim Trudeau were absolutely essential to this undertaking, as were Frank Donaldson and Victor Sullivan of the Warplane Research Group in Ireland. Without Sean's help, none of this would ever have happened. His tireless response to any of my requests was always delivered in the greatest and gentlest of spirit. Jim was equally as helpful, and went way out of his way to help me with this project. Their friendship is worth a thousand times the effort in writing this book.

In the West of Ireland, more people than I could possibly name helped me capture the feel of the lovely but often austere Connemara in World War II.

Towards the end of my journey, my friend Jeanne Anderson stepped up and pushed me at just the right time, with just the right amount of firmness.

More than anyone my wife, Wynnie, without exception, always encouraged me to continue along this path, particularly when things got tough. You're appreciated more than you know.

Here is a full list of the folks who helped me bring *Damnyankee* to the printed page:

Jeanne Anderson, Deb Barracato, Jeannette Boner, Jack Brady and his grandson Adam, J. Robb Brady, Jennifer Corona, Frank

Donaldson, Robert Emerson, Jerry Flecker, Lisa Jones of Outskirts Press, Sean Kelly, Maureen Kelly, Paud Kenneely, Carole Lusser, Sheila McDonough, Gabriel McNamara, Josie McNamara, Jimmy O'Malley, Karen Russell, Wayne Smith, Victor Sullivan, Jim Trudeau, Lyn Trudeau, Dorothy Vigeant, Wynne Ann Walsh, and Hill Goodspeed and Roger Mott of the National Museum of Naval Aviation of Pensacola, Florida.

CHAPTER I

A YANK ARRIVES IN CLIFDEN---1985

As Sean pushed his Fiat through Galway and on to R59, heading north into Connemara, a warm feeling of familiarity surged over him as he motored on towards Clifden with Maureen and their daughter Eimear, asleep in the back seat.

At the outset of the trip, they had dropped their son Brian off at St. Jarlath's college in Tuam, and then they drove south to see Sean's family in County Cork. Brian was 14, and doing well in school. Sean's visit with his mother and sisters in Coolea, West Cork, had been brilliant. As always, it felt good to be going home to beautiful little Clifden, tucked into Ardbear Bay along the coast of the Atlantic. Clifden was bordered to the west by the Atlantic, and to the east by the shadow of the brooding Maamturk Mountains in the sparsely populated West of Ireland.

September was one of Sean's favorite months. It was traditionally a dry, sunny month, as if it were God's little peace offering before the autumn rains came. After a few days away, though, he'd begun to feel a familiar sense of duty dragging his mind and heart back to his job as Sergeant for the Garda in the Clifden District. Weaving his way past Oughterard and heading for Maam Cross, Sean's weariness was offset by his sense of relief at heading back to his duties. Had he not felt so tired, he might have nosed the Fiat west at Screeb on R336 through Rossaveal towards Glinsk, Cashel Bay, Roundstone, and Ballyconneely on the coast route, rather than taking the more direct way back.

He had lived in Clifden more than 23 years, since his transfer from Burtonport in County Donegal. He never tired of seeing the wild Atlantic, launching an incessant attack upon the west coast, tirelessly pounding the shores, looking for an advantage, an opening that never quite came. Fatigue and the advancing hour, however, required he take the quicker inland route, which was still not lacking in beauty.

Sean had met Maureen in 1959, shortly after he was transferred up to Burtonport from Galway. He often wondered if there was something in the water up there in the wild north of Ireland that endowed the lasses with such good looks. A smile unwittingly crept over his face as he remembered his first sight of the red-tressed beauty, playing the organ in church. It was certainly little wonder that she had come under his notice! He cast a quick eye over to the seat next to him. Her beauty seemed only to have grown with the addition of her years of maturity. They had married in 1962, and relocated to the Clifden Garda post almost immediately.

He and Maureen had made a nice life in Clifden for themselves and their two children, Eimear, who was 12, and Brian, a couple years older. It was hard to believe they were so grown up. Where had the years gone?

Fifteen minutes or so after turning west on the Clifden road R59 at Maam Cross, Sean relaxed a bit, knowing it'd be only a short time before they motored through Clifden and up the hill towards home. They climbed Pat Nee's Hill past Clifden town, and Maureen began to waken Eimear just a turn or two before they entered their driveway. With school scheduled for the morrow, Maureen had timed the arousal so she could usher Eimear off to bed with a minimum of fuss.

After hauling the luggage into the front hall, Sean thought he'd better call the Garda station, both to let them know he was back and to see if there were any problems during his absence. He hoped the station had stayed quiet.

"Clifden Garda Station."

"Hello Siobhan, it's Sean, and I just called to let you know we are safely back. I'll be in bright and early in the morning. Would you take a few minutes then and bring me up to date?"

"Oh Sean, it's brilliant that you called just now. I've been taking calls all day from an American who absolutely insists that he must talk with you yet today." Sean's spirits sank. He was hoping for a quiet cup of tea in the garden as the sun dropped down past Ardbear Bay.

"Siobhan, can you ring him back and tell him I'll be in touch the very first thing in the morning? I've still to put away the things from the trip, and to tell you the truth, I was looking forward to getting a good rest before tomorrow. Surely a few hours delay won't harm a thing. If you would, go ahead and make an appointment with him in the morning, as early as possible, and I'll be there to see him. Do you know what this is about, and why it's so pressing?"

"Oh Sean, I'm afraid that won't do. The American was most insistent that he talk with you tonight, as they are leaving for America tomorrow. Flying out of Shannon, they are, and he said it's most urgent that he speak with you yet today. They are staying at the Abbeyglen Castle Hotel, and he said they could be reached all evening. They will wait in their room to hear from you."

"Siobhan, did he state the nature of this emergency that couldn't wait until the morrow?"

"Well Sean, he said something about an airplane crash near Clifden, but I didn't get much else out of the man. He was polite enough, but there was no question that yer man wanted to speak with the head of the Garda. It seemed that nothing else would serve him."

"Thanks Siobhan, I'll ring the Abbeyglen as soon as we're off." Sean wondered what this was all about. To the best of his knowledge, there hadn't been any airplane crash around Clifden for several years.

"Hello Seamus, this is Sean Kelly. Do you have a Mr. Vigeant, an American, staying with you?"

"Oh surely Sean, I do, I do. And it's not like yer man isn't waiting to talk with you."

"Could you ring his suite, please Seamus?"

The phone was picked up after a single ring.

"Ed Vigeant here, is this Sergeant Kelly?"

Before Sean could answer, the man continued.

"Sergeant Kelly, it's vitally important that I talk with you tonight, even if only for a few minutes. My wife and I must leave for the United States tomorrow afternoon. It seems like you're my last hope."

"Mr. Vigeant, I've only returned from a trip to the south. Is this something that couldn't wait until the first thing in the morning?"

"Sergeant Kelly, it's a matter of great urgency to me, and I'd very much like a few minutes of your time tonight. Could you meet me and my wife in the hotel lounge in say, twenty minutes?"

Sean surprised himself. "Very well Mr. Vigeant, I shall see you in twenty minutes."

He had heard a click on the other end the minute he'd agreed to the meeting. Well, the tea and the muse in the garden would have to await another day, Sean thought. He pulled on a jacket and took the keys from the hook in the hallway.

Sean entered the lounge at the Glen and greeted the barkeep. "Hello Jimmy, and how are you keeping yourself tonight?"

"Well Sean, and sure if it isn't good to see you back! There's an American...." Before Jimmy could finish, a husky middle-aged man jumped up from the table where he was sitting with a woman in the sparsely populated lounge and strode purposely across the floor.

"Sergeant Kelly, I'm Ed Vigeant." The American extending his hand with a viselike grip, with his other hand on Sean's shoulder, he guided him towards the table. "Sergeant Kelly, this is my wife, Dorothy. We both want to thank you for being kind enough to meet us here. We know you are probably tired from your trip, but this simply couldn't wait."

Sean greeted Mrs. Vigeant, using her married name and thinking what a pleasant-looking woman she was as he took the offered hand. Vigeant asked Sean what he would like to drink, and Sean nodded at Jimmie, who immediately busied himself by pouring a lemon drink over a glass full of ice. Sean couldn't help remembering that it wasn't so many years ago that ice was a rarity in the West of Ireland, and that drinks were served over a tumbler of it in only the toniest of places; now he felt thirsty, though, and welcomed the cool lemon drink.

"Thank you, Mr. Vigeant. As you can see, I'm a man of habit, and unfortunately Jimmy knows most of them. It's a pleasure to meet you both and I must ask how may I help you. It's obvious that there's a great sense of urgency in your mission, whatever it might be."

"Yes, there is, and it's fueled by the fact that we have to catch a late afternoon plane out of Shannon to return to New York. Our tickets wouldn't allow us to change without great additional expense. We've been here a week and have been pretty frustrated with what we are looking for. I was told that if anyone could help us, it would be Sean Kelly. Had we known about you, and that you were going to be on vacation, we'd have come a little later."

"Exactly what is it you want my help with, Mr. Vigeant?"

"Well, Sergeant Kelly, I'm trying to obtain information about an airplane crash near Ballyconneely and have had very little success. I've been to the school, the Garda Station, and the Clifden Hospital, and so far, nobody has been able to help. Paud Kenneely, the retired school principal down in Ailleabreach, told me that if anyone could help, it would be you."

"Well now, sometimes Paud is too kindly, and gives me more credit than might be due, I'm afraid. Tell me, was this crash fairly recent? My memory tells me that we haven't had a crash in the Connemara area for several years now."

The American laughed, "Oh no, this crash happened in the fall of 1944 during the war. It was forty-one years ago. You see, I was on that plane when we ditched it at sea."

Sean looked at Vigeant with more than a little surprise on his face.

"Mr. Vigeant, are you sure it was around Clifden? I've been here for a long time, more than twenty years, and I must say I've never heard of such an incident. Are you sure of the area?"

Vigeant laughed again, "Oh yeah, I'm sure. That isn't the kind of thing that you forget very easily, particularly when it happens to you when you're only eighteen years old."

Sean looked at his watch, and then turned to the pleasant American couple.

"Mr. and Mrs. Vigeant, would it be possible for you to meet me quite early in the morning at the Garda station, let's say around 8 a.m.? I'd be better prepared to take a more detailed statement from you there than I am tonight. If I'm to be of any help, I'd like to be able to get as much information as possible. Would that be too early for you?"

"Are you kidding? Heck no, that'd be fine. I've waited forty-plus years for this, and I'm not about to let an extra half hour of sleep get in my way."

The three rose and shook hands good night. Sean walked out the door, nodding to his friend Jimmy.

Vigeant looked at Dorothy and said, "You know honey, for some reason I think we just hit a home run. I've got a feeling that Mr. Sean

Kelly is the answer we're looking for. Don't ask me why, but I think this fellow is going to be able to help us. It's just a hunch, but I think he's our man."

"Eddie, for your sake, I hope you're right. I know how much this means to you. Now let's go get some sleep, as tomorrow could be a big day. We want to be sharp when we sit down with Sergeant Kelly. I had a little hunch of my own. He seems like a good man, and a fellow that will help us, if there's help to be had."

CHAPTER II

A TALE FROM FORTY YEARS BEFORE

The next morning, Sean met the Vigeants at the Garda station. He couldn't help but like them. Like so many other Americans he'd met while they were visiting Ireland, they oozed enthusiasm and friendliness. After setting the Vigeants up in a little meeting room, Sean disappeared momentarily, then reappeared, armed with a paper pad and several pens.

"Mr. Vigeant, if you don't mind, I think the best way for us to operate is for me to take as many notes as possible as we speak. This will give me a better chance to react, if in fact we are to find out more about your adventure. Initially I will ask you a number of very routine questions, including name, address, and so forth. While this might seem time-consuming, my experience at these matters tells me that one cannot get too much basic information."

"Sean, however you want to proceed is fine with me."

Sean felt a little embarrassed that Vigeant used his first name so freely, but he nonetheless found he liked the American.

"To begin with, I, Sean Kelly, Sergeant at the Clifden, Galway Garda station, am taking a deposition from an American, today, Tuesday, the 17TH of September, 1985. Please state your full name and where you are from."

"Joseph Edward Vigeant, of Wynantskill, New York."

Sean scribbled briefly and resumed his questions.

"Please tell me about yourself."

Vigeant told Sean that he was born in Hudson, New York, to a mother and father of Irish and French descent, respectively. He had joined the United States Navy, Naval Aviation group, in September of 1942, at the age of 16.

Vigeant then told the story of an American Navy plane, with a crew of ten that left Norfolk, Virginia, in September, 1944. Enroute

9

to England, via the northern route through Labrador and Iceland, the plane was blown off course by bad weather; radio problems, and some malfunctioning gear contributed to what was already a bad situation. After about sixteen hours in the air and running short on fuel, the pilot was forced to ditch at sea. Four of the crew perished during the perilous maneuver in the stormy Atlantic and another died in the life raft. After more than two nights adrift without food or water, the remaining five, along with the corpse of the crewmate who died in the dinghy, drifted ashore at Ailleabreach, near Ballyconneely, a little fishing village on the coast of Galway.

Vigeant wove a fascinating story about the pilot and himself, being the only two with any strength left at all, stumbling out on the beach and literally crawling to first one home, where they were not received, and finally to a little fishing cottage, where they were taken in. There, they were administered to, while others went to help the remaining crew on the beach. As soon as possible, the survivors were all transported by lorry ambulance to the Clifden Cottage Hospital, where they recovered from their ordeal.

After about a week of convalescing, the Americans were transported to the border of Northern Ireland, where they were handed over to a single American officer. A wake was held for the deceased sailor, a good friend of Vigeant's, in a Church of Ireland ceremony in Clifden, and his body was taken to Northern Ireland for interment. After a week or so at a hospital in Northern Ireland, the five survivors were flown to England, and after a couple of weeks in London, they all returned to America.

As Sean continued to take down as many details as possible while Vigeant spoke, he couldn't help but wonder why he had never heard this story before. He prided himself on having kept a good ear as to the history of his Clifden-Connemara area of responsibility, but this was the first he had heard of such a thing.

After several hours, Sean felt he had a fairly comprehensive accounting of the story. He asked the American why this was of such importance to him.

"There are no existing records of this flight in the records of the U.S. Navy, at least as far as I was able to find. If I could find verification on this side of the Atlantic, somehow, it would greatly help any of the five of us still alive to gain admittance to any

American veteran's hospital on a priority basis, if the need were to arise. I should say *when* the need comes, as none of us are getting any younger," Vigeant pointed out.

Sean asked Vigeant to sign it, which he did promptly.

"Is there anything at all that you might have which would help lend credibility to your quest?"

"Only this, Sergeant Kelly."

Vigeant fished in his jacket pocket, and withdrew a small, well-worn black-and-white photograph. "Someone took this and gave me a copy just before we were taken from Clifden and brought to the border of Northern Ireland."

The photo was of five young men standing and sitting around a young woman wearing the white cap of a nurse. Four of the men had slight smiles on their faces, with the fellow sitting in the foreground looking exhausted, and not in good health.

Sean studied the picture for several long moments, and slowly handed it back to the American.

"Well, Mr. and Mrs.Vigeant, it's been a pleasure meeting you both and I have to say your story sounds fascinating. While I cannot tell you I'll be able to help directly, I will tell you that I'll try, and I will use whatever tools are at my disposal to see if I can find anything for you. With your permission, I will have a copy made of your photo here at the station. It may be helpful if we are able to move this investigation forward. I've taken your address, so that if I am able to uncover anything I'll be able to write you, and let you know of any outcome."

He looked at his watch.

"Better get on your way now. Traffic has increased in Connemara, as well as in Galway; I shouldn't think you'd want to wait much longer before beginning your journey. If you leave within the next fifteen minutes or so, you should arrive at Shannon before your flight."

They all shook hands, and Sean ushered the American couple from the station towards their rental car.

Sean immersed himself in the details of his job, getting a feel for what of significance had happened during his holiday from Clifden. The Vigeants kept popping up in the back of his mind, though, distracting him as he pored over activity reports of the last week.

It began to get annoying. How could he help these folks? If they hadn't been able to turn up anything through police records, the hospital, and even from Paud Kenneelly down in Ballyconneely, what new could he provide? How could he find proof that a group of men had risen up out of the sea, in this remote little corner of Ireland, over forty years ago? Maybe the photo would shed some light on the situation. He sighed, shook his head clear, and went back to his work.

That evening over tea, Sean recounted his meeting with the Vigeants to Maureen.

"Sean, that's a fascinating tale. In a way it's a wonderful story, but in another way, very sad. I imagine those men were really nothing much more than lads, were they? I wonder why he waited so long to try and piece it back together?"

"I don't know, Maureen, but he did say that he needed to be able to verify his story to show some form of continuity of service. Apparently there is a blank spot in his war record, and he mentioned that, without being able to fill this in, he and other members of the crew could encounter difficulties obtaining medical help in the States, if they needed it.

"At any rate, I'd like to be able to help, as they seemed to be good people. I just don't know quite where to begin."

"Well Sean, if I know you, and I'm pretty sure I do after all these years, if there's a way to help them, you're the man able to find it."

Sean smiled as he began to clear the dishes. If he were as capable as Maureen seemed to think he was, there should be no problem here. He only wished he could be as confident as Maureen.

CHAPTER III

MAUREEN TAKES HER EVENING WALK

Maureen finished washing the dishes, tossed her apron on the counter, grabbed her rain slicker off the wall peg and headed out the door for her habitual evening walk. She very much looked forward to closing her day this way, as it allowed her to enjoy the beauty of Clifden. Maureen had never quite got over missing the wonderful, blustery wildness of her childhood home in County Donegal. Having grown up in the little fishing village of Burtonport, Maureen felt a bit detached if she were ever too far from the sea. While County Galway wasn't quite as primordial as Donegal, this was a lovely part of the west coast of Ireland.

This evening, clouds were scudding down the coast from the north. While the sky grew darker, Maureen hoped she'd finish her walk before the squall touched down on The Faul Road, which wound westward past their home until it met the bay, Maureen's favorite spot on her usual route. She always enjoyed the prospect of seeing the sea at the end of the road.

Maureen was a teacher. Things had been going well for her at the Ballyconneely National School; this year's class of children seemed to be doing well with their Irish-language class. Many in Ireland felt preserving the national language was a lost cause, but Maureen resisted that idea fiercely. She felt deeply that their native language needed to be saved. She felt she could somehow help sear their very Irishness into the souls of the children she taught.

She felt the very lilt and intonation of Irish held a beauty of its own. She never tired of the almost mystical sound of the Celtic words and phrases. If ever a language was created to represent the soft beauty of its homeland, it was Irish, she thought.

Maureen snapped out of her reverie to notice the wind had picked up, and a lashing of real rain began. Hard rain. Driving rain.

The squall had hit, and as was not unusual in the West of Ireland, with amazing force. She quickly darted down a side lane to Tom and Mary Gavin's house. In a lighter rain she would have persevered homeward, but this storm looked a bit nasty. Besides, she always enjoyed the company of her friends.

"Maureen, Maureen, come in out of that awful weather before you drown. What ever put you out on an evening like this? You didn't do something now to anger the gods, did you Maureen?"

"Oh now Tom, I don't think so, but thanks for having me in until this blows over." Maureen took her soggy slicker off and hung it on a peg in the entryway.

"Well Maureen, aren't you a sight for sore eyes, and won't you enjoy a nice cup of tea with Tom and me, and dry out by the fire." Mary threw a dish towel over her shoulder as she came in from the kitchen.

"Sit down over here and dry out. I'll put the pot on the cooker, and we'll all enjoy a nice cup of tea and a wee chat. It seems like I haven't seen you in years now, so we've some catching up to do. How is Sean holding up, and how was your trip down to Cork?"

Maureen smiled. To her friend Mary, a week or two could well seem like years, when it came to missing her friends.

Mary's voice faded slightly as she drifted back into the kitchen. Maureen settled into a soft chair, relaxing for the moment, and taking in the familiar peaty aroma of the Gavins' fire. The truth be, the glow of the fire felt and looked wonderful. Nothing smelled better than a Connemara turf fire, particularly on a wet night. It seemed the very essence of the West of Ireland, and Maureen loved to smell the heather, the moisture, and the pure Irishness of the dried turf. Mary reappeared shortly, pleased to see that Maureen had settled in next to the fireplace.

"Now Maureen, what is new with you and Sean?" Mary asked.

"Well, we had a brilliant visit with Sean's mother and his sisters down in Cork, but I'll have to say, it's nice to be home again, Mary. It's also quite nice to be drying out next to your fire, and to see the two of you again."

Maureen accepted the cup of tea Mary handed her, and began to tell the Gavins of Sean's encounter with the Americans the night they returned home. She recounted how the American couple had so insisted on seeing Sean that very night. She repeated the story Sean had told her---how this American, who had been little more than a boy at the time, recounted the story of this awful, grueling ordeal at sea, and how one of his mates had died in the bottom of the life raft, unable to continue the fight against terrible conditions, only hours before they washed ashore at Ailleabreach.

Tom understood the implications.

"Glory be to God, and think what would have happened to them had they not washed ashore at that little spit of a beach? Why, they would have shot back out to sea, and would have been lucky to have washed up on the Aran Islands days later, if at all."

Maureen continued with the story, as best she could recall, telling about the Americans' recovery in the Clifden hospital, then being whisked away to the north of Ireland.

"And Maureen, how can it be that the hospital, nor the Garda Station, or even the Church has no record of this?"

"Mary, I don't know, but it's a good guess that things were jumbled up around here forty years ago, during the war. And sure isn't it true that folks probably had a full-time job just keeping alive in the west of Ireland during the '40s, let alone keeping good records of what went on during the war.

"Well, I have to tell you it was wonderful seeing you both, and now that it looks like the skies have lifted a bit, I'll be on my way home again. Sean will be wondering if I was drowned, or swept out to sea. Mary, thank you so kindly, and I'll look forward to seeing you in church on Sunday."

The following morning was sprinkled with an ever-so-light mist. Sean had to run down to Ailleabreach on business, and thought he might drop in on one or two of the old fellows in the village, to see if he could kick up any dust about the Vigeant tale.

As Sean moved on down the coast road towards Ailleabreach, the mist began to lift, as it did so often as a morning progressed. As he passed the old Alcock and Brown historical site, where two American aviators had landed in 1919, marking the world's first transatlantic flight, Sean felt his spirits lifting. It would be a fine day, and he always enjoyed traveling down the coast.

CHAPTER IV

THE FRIENDSHIP OF OLIVE AND TOMMY

A few days after Maureen's brief visit, Tom and Mary Gavin were having afternoon tea with their son Thomas, a fine lad of 16. Tom was grateful for the boy's sunny disposition, and the fact that he had never been anything but a joy to the two of them.

"Thomas, would you have another helping of Colcannon?"

"Yes Mum, there's still enough room left in me stomach for one more helping. 'Tis awfully good."

"Thomas, did you hear the story Mrs. Kelly dropped in here with the other night?"

Tom Senior told his son about an American airplane going down at sea during the war.

He was only about a third of the way through the tale of the men crashing into the sea when young Thomas dropped his knife and fork.

"Mum, Miss Harley---Olive Harley---knew those men!"

"Tommy, whatever are you talking about? What do you mean?"

Thomas had been doing odd jobs for quite some time to help out Miss Harley, a maiden lady who lived down the road just as you entered Clifden. Olive Harley had always treated Thomas kindly, and they had developed a solid friendship, despite the enormous difference in their ages. Over the years their relationship had grown and flourished, similar to that of a grandmother and her grandchild.

Olive had never married. Perhaps he was the child she may have yearned to have raised.

Their friendship was built around books. Young Thomas Gavin had a true love for books, and had ever since he was a lad. Olive loved to read as well, and through her life had accumulated an impressive little library. Thomas was more than welcome to delve into her books. Delve he had, and some of their grandest times together were spent in her little library, when the two of them sat down on occasional afternoons, with tea and cakes Olive had made. At those times, they talked at length about books and various authors they had read. Thomas had grown to love those sessions, and the fondness Olive felt toward him was certainly returned.

"Mum, Olive knew those men. I saw them in her autograph book!"

"Thomas, what are you talking about? What autograph book?"

"Olive has a book, an old, gray book, quite worn out, 'tis. She had it when she was just a lass, and has kept it all these years. I looked through it from time to time, and she knew of course, and didn't care a bit.

"I remember a number of times seeing a photo from the war of a number of young soldiers, Americans, sitting on the steps outside the Clifden Hospital. Olive knew them all, and said they were fine lads. Every last one of them, she said.

"Sometimes when we looked at the book, she seemed almost sad for a moment, but the moment always passed quickly. Their airplane had crashed off the coast during the war, and they were taken to the Clifden Hospital to recover, before they were sent away. She worked as a Red Cross volunteer during the war, and helped take care of them. She had each one of them autograph her book, right where she kept the picture. I saw it, Mum, many times."

"Well now, Thomas, I'm sure you did, and isn't it grand Olive shared that with you?

Later that evening, Mary and Tom discussed the revelation from their son.

"Migod Mary, is that the truth? I wonder why Thomas never mentioned it to us?"

"Well Tom, and why would he? It's not as if he were hiding anything from us. You know the boy and Olive are wonderful friends, and I'm sure it's just one of those things that he's known about for some time. The next time we see the Kellys, we'll have to tell them for sure. Maybe it'll help Sean with the Americans. That might help him with their research."

"Yes Mary, I'm sure it could. I'm sure it could."

Almost a fortnight passed before the Gavins were to see either Sean or Maureen. Willie Mulkerrin, a bachelor in the parish in his early 80's, needed a bit of help putting up his hay. Sean Kelly, Tom Gavin, Kevin Stanley and Michael Gaoghan all decided to lend Willie a hand.

Not realizing Maureen had already spoken with the Gavins about his strange visit with the Americans, Sean mentioned the story to Tom.

"Sean, and don't you know, I forgot that Maureen told us that story not a fortnight ago. I plumb forgot about it, I did. You know, we mentioned it to young Thomas, as it was such an interesting tale. Sure and didn't he tell us that Olive knew those lads!"

"What? Tom, tell me again what you just said."

"Well Sean, you know that Olive and Mary have been friends for years. Young Thomas has helped her out for a number of years with little chores, and they've become fast friends as well. You know, Olive is one terror of a reader. She can read a book in the time it takes most folks to open the cover. Young Tom isn't far behind, and I believe he and Olive have shared many a book together."

"But Tom, what does this have to do with the story of the American aviators?"

"Well now Sean, let's not get ahead of ourselves. As it turns out, Olive worked as a Red Cross volunteer in the war, and she served some duty in the Clifden hospital, she did. Olive, it seems, kept an autograph book, as did a lot of young lasses in those times. Thomas has seen it several times, and had noticed more than once there was a photo of a bunch of young American chaps, flyers they were, and they were shot down, or crashed, or something off the coast, and didn't the Army bring them to Clifden to recuperate a bit? Olive helped tend to them, and she told Thomas they were a fine bunch of lads, each and every one of them. They, to a man, signed her autograph book."

Sean could hardly wait to get out of there, and see if he could find Olive Harley, but he had to spend a few moments with Willie, accepting his heartfelt thanks for the help with the haying. He realized he'd have to put Olive's visit off until the morning.

CHAPTER V

OLIVE'S AUTOGRAPH BOOK

The following morning, after calling the Garda station to let them know he'd be coming in late, Sean headed straightaway over to see Olive Harley. A smile stole across his face as he pulled up in front of her two-story, red brick terrace house on Riverside Street, across the road from the River Owenglenn, and just below the town of Clifden. She kept the place neat and charming. It wasn't a grand house in size, Sean thought, but Olive maintained it perfectly, which is what one would expect of her. She was a lovely person, and had done well in her life; her list of friends would cover many a sheet of paper.

The door opened after only a couple of raps. As soon as Olive saw Sean, a wonderful smile crept across her face.

"Well now, Sean Kelly, and I suppose you've come to drag me off to jail, have you Sean? Pray tell me, what have I done wrong to merit a visit from the Garda?"

Sean laughed, and said, "Oh Olive, if everyone about Clifden behaved as well as you, I'd have no job at all now, would I?"

As Olive hustled Sean into the parlor, she was already on her way to the kitchen, talking over her shoulder.

"Take a seat now Sean, and let me put the kettle on. I haven't seen you in awhile, and it'll be grand hearing what you've been up to. And how is that lovely girl Maureen doing? I haven't seen her in weeks."

She scurried around the kitchen for a few moments, then re-entered the parlor. "Sean, the cooker is on, and we'll have a fine cup of tea in just a minute or so. It surely is good to see you, but again I have to ask, how was I blessed to find one of Ireland's finest on my stoop this beautiful morning?"

"Olive, I hope I don't ever need a real reason to stop by and say hello to such a fine friend as you. As a matter of fact, I do have something I may need your help with."

Sean related the story of his meeting with the Vigeants, filling her in as thoroughly as possible. She interrupted only long enough to fetch the teapot and some sweet cakes. He finished off by relaying his conversation with Tom Gavin the day before at Willie Mulkerrins' place.

"Olive, I told Mr. Vigeant I'd help him with his quest, and of course, after talking with Tom yesterday, I wanted to come and see you, and see what you could help me with. Is the story of the autograph book true?"

Olive sat for a moment, a far away look in her eyes. Then she turned slowly to Sean.

"Oh Sean, it 'tis, it 'tis. That was so long ago, and I was still fairly young then. Here, let me see if I can find it."

She rose and walked across the room, and in just a moment bent over and picked a book off the shelf.

"Sure and here it is. This old book has been sitting here with great patience hasn't it now, for over forty years. Sean, that's a long time now, isn't it?"

Sean nodded his agreement, and he reached for the book she handed him. He opened it to a page with a small black and white photo. There, plain as day was the picture of five young American lads, the same one Eddie Vigeant had shown him! The young men were sitting on the stoop outside the Clifden hospital. Four of them looked fairly happy, but the fifth, sitting in the foreground, looked a touch older. He also appeared to be in pain, and had a brooding look on his face. They were dressed in Irish clothes, somewhat ill-fitting but fully serviceable. As he turned the page, he found five separate pages, each carrying a single signature. In various scrawls of handwriting he read the following:

To Olive- From a grateful Yank. Gerald Flecker. 9-18-44.

To Olive- With best wishes. Frank P. Cicero.

Sept. 18, 1944, Joseph Edward Vigeant. RFD # 2, Newturn Pike Road. North Troy, New York.

Wilbur D. Lyle. 9-18-44.

To Olive-Who arrived hand in hand with God and Ireland to welcome us from the sea. James O. Trudeau.

Sean stared at the book, looking back and forth from the picture to the individual signatures. He could scarcely believe it. What must those young lads have gone through?

He turned to Olive. Her eyes were distant, and Sean saw the beginning of a tear welling up in them.

"Oh Olive, this is quite something now, isn't it? All of these years you've kept this book. Now one of those men has come back, and I think you'll be able to help me to help him. Isn't that grand?"

"Yes Sean, I believe I'll be able to help them, and I want to. I surely want to. They were fine young men. They were so exhausted and so sick when we saw them, but they surely were fine young men."

Olive gathered her composure, and in a moment the lovely, warm smile that people so admired reappeared on her face.

"Now Sean, exactly what is it that I can do to help Mr. Vigeant?"

"Well Olive, why don't we just sit here and you can write down your recollections of those days in the Clifden hospital? I've got a pad here, and maybe I can help you a bit if you need it."

Sean wrote at the top of the page: "Statement of Miss Olive Harley, Riverside, Clifden, made at her home on Sunday, 29th September, 1985, to Sergeant Sean Kelly, Clifden."

Olive took the policeman's pad, and sitting across from Sean, thought for a moment or two. She slowly began to write, stopping on occasion to gaze off to the distance. Then she would snap back into the present, and once again write on the little tablet.

"I am 75 years of age. I have lived in Clifden all my life. During the 1939-1945 war I was a member of the Clifden branch of the Red Cross, with the rank of Sergeant. I remember September, 1944, when six men, one of them dead, came ashore on a raft at Ailleabreach, Ballyconneely, less than ten miles from Clifden. I was called out early in the morning with others in the ambulance to bring the five survivors to Clifden hospital. I cannot remember what became of the body of the deceased. I used to visit the five survivors at Clifden hospital from time to time. I cannot remember how long they were kept at Clifden hospital. Each one of them gave me his autograph in my autograph book which I still have. I am now handing my autograph book over to Sergeant Kelly. The names of the five survivors in my autograph book are as follows: James O. Trudeau, Wilbur D. Lyle (dated September 18, 1944), Gerald Flecker (dated September 18, 1944), Frank P. Cicero, Joseph Edward Vigeant (dated September 18, 1944). I must have received all five autographs on the same date as the two undated ones are in between pages dated September 18th, 1944. This statement has been read over to me and it is correct. Signed, Olive Harley."

Sean then briefly added to the notebook, Witnessed: S. Kelly, Sergeant 10502G.

"There Olive, and didn't you do a grand job with this business? I appreciate this very much, and I know Mr. Vigeant will as well."

"Oh Sean, this is the least I can do for those poor dear men. Now where do we go from here?"

"Well Olive, if you've the time, I'd like to transport you down to the Garda station, where we can have this typed up as an official affidavit, and have it signed once more by yourself, and then notarized. Would you have the time to do that now, Olive?"

"Oh, I'm sure I can find the time now, Sean," Olive said, laughing. "What else would I be doing? Besides, it'll be quite a sight, you taking me into the Garda station. That should give folks something to talk about for a few days now, at the very least. Let me just get my jumper, and we'll be off to the station."

A stenographer there typed Olive's written statement. Sean dictated a final addition, to make it official, and attached the photostat copies of the autographs. Then they headed to the Notary's and the day's business was done, with Olive none the worse for wear.

CHAPTER VI

A NEW CREW MEETS A NEW AIRCRAFT

In late summer 1944, shipshape in clean, pressed blue denim fatigues, the Navy airmen moved slowly and methodically around the plane, saying nothing, taking in everything, and checking her out as if she were some kind of prey. They took her in with great care, squinting in the bright Virginia sun, her clear plastic Erco nose turret reflecting their faces.

She was immense in white and gray, an immaculate, brand-new "PB4Y-1," the latest, most advanced model off the line, they had been told. The letters identified her as a Patrol Bomber, in the fourth modification from the original design, with "Y" being the code for her creator, Consolidated Aircraft of San Diego. It was a version of a bomber popularly referred to as a "Liberator."

From this day on, their second on the long-established, sprawling Norfolk Navy Base, they were the seven enlisted sailors who, along with three officers, would operate this fighting machine. How formidable she looked. The feelings welling up inside them were complex: a swirling confusion of awe and pride, and yes, fear. Fear because as awesome as she appeared, she also symbolized the unknown that lay ahead.

Jim Trudeau saw her differently. As her pilot and at 26 years old the senior crewmember in rank and age, she and everything and everyone aboard her would be his responsibility. He was a U.S. Navy Lieutenant, Junior Grade, average height, average weight, pretty much "average everything," as he described himself with more conviction than modesty. Like his men, he was dressed for the occasion. He wore "working tans," one of five different uniforms American Naval aviators were entitled to wear--no jacket, a shirt with a lone single bar on the collar points. The Navy provided no insignia for the additional designation "PPC" for Patrol Plane

Commander. It was one of those "you-know-damned-well-who-you-are" titles familiar to the military, and its literal meaning was "captain of the ship."

Trudeau cast one more long look at her, then ducked and made his way under the plane's belly to the bomb bay hatch. He peered up into the dark, and shouted "Snave!"

That would be Carl Snavely, his co-pilot.

"Yo, boss," came the reply from the bowels of the aircraft. "You got the keys?"

"Nope, Old Booger gave 'em to you yesterday," Trudeau replied.

"I know, but the SOB had only one key, and I gave it to Wilbur. I guess he opened her up. Old Booger is supposed to give us everything we need. So far we've got just about half of everything, including the keys. You better stomp on him."

Trudeau shook off the thought. "Sorry Snave, he outranks me, as you damned well know. I'm afraid he's our liaison officer for keeps. He's still pissed off because I told him we wouldn't fly unless the number four oil gauge got fixed. Let's hope we don't need him for anything else from now on."

Snavely's mouth fell open. "You mean we have this SOB until we take off for England?"

"Yup. Hang in there. I'm coming aboard." Trudeau grabbed the handles on either side of the hatch and swung himself up, legs first, landing on the inner deck, four feet up.. "Jesus, no wonder the Navy makes us do all those friggin' pushups."

Trudeau climbed up onto the flight deck and slid into the first pilot's seat on the left side of the cockpit. His co-pilot was Ensign Carl Grey Snavely Jr., a big kid from Ithaca, New York. Trudeau thought Snave was an excellent co-pilot, and felt fortunate to have him. They met for the first time at Chincoteague. Snave and his wife Helen had arrived in an eyebrow-raising wartime rarity, a new convertible. Six feet tall with the round, ruddy face of a Minnesota farm boy, he bore a famous name: every American college football fan knew of Carl Snavely, head coach at Cornell University. Trudeau's co-pilot was his adopted son.

Having played football himself at Ohio University, Trudeau felt an early twinge of distinction at his unexpected adjacency to fame, but soon began to feel uneasy about it. Eyes in high places were bound to be focused on the younger Snavely, and Trudeau was struck by the thought that every move he made might be closely watched. Was Snavely Junior the kind of guy who might write nitpicking mail to the folks back home? Trudeau had seen this dance played out before, as a flight instructor at Pensacola. In letters to the home front, guys who washed out frequently blamed their failure on a particular check pilot or instructor.

He soon learned, however, that young Snavely was a regular guy. Oh, from time to time he might have taken his commissioned rank a bit too seriously, like most freshly minted Ensigns, but that would wear off quickly, Trudeau knew. At the core the kid was tough, realistic, eager to learn, a hard worker. He had earned a degree in hotel management at Cornell, contrary to the prevailing assumption that he would naturally follow physical education and coaching. With that, Snave demonstrated a mind of his own; he would follow orders, but was able to go "beyond the book" if the rulebook somehow came up short.

"Everybody on board?" Trudeau asked.

"I am, Skip, you can't go anywhere without me," another voice rang out.

Ensign Phil Mills was another matter. Tall and handsome with a bit of swagger, he had a tough outer shell, cultivated in his hometown Chicago. The enlisted men were naturally drawn to him, as they recognized something of themselves in him, and he fell in easily with their banter. This all counted on the plus side with Trudeau, who himself had seen enough of the mean streets of large cities. One thing did concern him about Mills, however. By 1944, the Navy had found itself with a plethora of fledgling fliers who had graduated from the demanding schools of naval aviation. Suddenly, thousands of qualified young pilots were unceremoniously sent to a "navigators pool" for training as full-time, non-flying navigators. This would allow them to maintain their flight status when more pilots were required, while allowing the Navy access to the extensive navigation skills these lads had received as part of the requirement for being awarded naval aviator wings.

Trudeau realized Mills had become embittered over losing the chance to hold "the stick" in his hands; he appeared to hate the reality of being relegated to the navigator's table aft of the flight deck. His bitterness began to show itself in demands for multi-engine training at a time when Trudeau himself was just beginning to swap the arcane techniques of handling "flying boats" for the different but equally complex skills required to fly heavy, land-based aircraft. Trudeau could not help but feel sympathy for Mills. He would have railed at the system himself if, after all that training, the personal high that comes with earning those wings and learning how to fly, some suit in Washington decided he would simply have to watch other guys at the controls.

Ensign Mills was frustrated at being "downsized"---his term---to navigator. There were simply too many pilots in the Navy and many of them were assigned to other duties. Mills was none too happy about his situation; he had his wings, he'd earned them like everyone else, and he flat wanted to fly. Trudeau understood. Guys at this level wouldn't be as good as they were without that competitive edge. He would do whatever he could to alleviate the young officer's disappointment but didn't think there was an awful lot he could do about it.

"Wouldn't want to go anywhere without you, Mister," Trudeau said. "Incidentally, did you get rid of the Missus?"

"What a crude way to put it, Skip. Yup, I put her on the train to ol' Chicago last night."

"Tearful?"

"You bet."

"It ain't easy. You should have sent her packing earlier when Snave and I did, at Chincoteague."

"Hell, you guys just don't love your wives the way I do."

Snavely smiled. "Phil, I didn't know you loved our wives. You know, I always suspected you were somewhat of a predator."

They went on like that while Trudeau got comfortable in the pilot's seat. In front of him was a massive array of instruments, 27 of them as a matter of fact, all designed to help fly and monitor the flight of this heavy bomber. Twelve levers were placed between the seats for the pilot and copilot, to control throttle feed, fuel/air mix, propeller pitch, turbocharger boost and more for this four-engine monster of a plane.

Trudeau turned to look at his co-pilot. "Carl, let's check the crew at their stations."

"Just a minute." Snavely held up a finger for silence. "It's the tower. Damn, we've got a hold. There's an emergency coming in. We gotta wait."

"Well, Carl, while we're waiting, I've got something to tell you."

"Oh?"

"Yeah. We've got a name." Trudeau laughed. The boys had been arguing over a name for a week. *"Damnyankee!"*

"You're kidding…"

"Hell no, I'm not kidding. We're all from up north, they figure. Yeah. *Damnyankee*. With the 'n' after 'm' no less. I hope like hell we can get away with it."

"Why not? It's a great name."

"First, it won't be official until we get the green light from upstairs. Second, no name, of anything---any outfit or piece of gear--- is supposed to suggest its origin or where it came from, or where it might be going."

Mills joined the party. "What's *Damnyankee* got to do with that kind of stuff? Sounds harmless to me."

"Well," Trudeau said, "it suggests where the crew came from. You'd be surprised at the information the Krauts might use. Look, let's just assume that's the name. It's a great name. We'll keep it until somebody takes it away from us. Even then we'll keep it. For ourselves."

So the officers and crew of the newly-named *Damnyankee* sat on the tarmac, and Trudeau stared at the flight plan he'd already read a dozen times. He was growing sleepy.

"You guys speak softly, 'cause I'm gonna get some shuteye. Wake me up when that pigeon comes home to roost," he said. Trudeau took off his cap and let his thoughts wander. Soon his mind was spreading pictures of his men across the sheet, just as they had looked when he first met them. That was back at Chincoteague, a place of long runways slashed across a little Virginia island famed for wild ponies they never saw. Looking back, he felt the same surge of pride he had known then, for their very presence at "Chinco" made them a select group. "Chinco" was more than just another naval air station: among other distinctions, it was the first step for select crews earmarked for training in highly classified equipment and tactics. Trudeau considered himself lucky to be there, even if it meant Atlantic duty instead of the Pacific, which everybody he knew seemed to prefer. Lots of submarine patrol pilots felt their function would be better served in the Pacific, as the Army Air Corps had already been pretty active in the Atlantic. Besides, the Pacific was warmer in case you got dunked.

Trudeau knew his two officers better than the seven others of his crew. They'd all been working like dogs with training, which kept them going from dawn until they flopped into bed at night. Getting to know the enlisted men was next to impossible when they were actually in the air. He had tried on a number of occasions to wander aft to shoot the breeze with them, but his voice was no match for the rush of air, the roar and rattle of equipment, and just general banging around that accompanied any flight of a PB4Y-1. She was big, she was blustery. She didn't do demure very well.

A second barrier was the nature of the Navy itself: democracy was left at the gate, something for the civilian, peace-time world. Officers had complete freedom to fraternize with other officers, but it was "off-limits" to cross the social line with the men in the enlisted ranks. It was a general rule in the military everywhere; personal relationships could compromise discipline.

The PB4Y-1 roster numbered ten, so that meant seven besides himself, Snavely and Mills.

Trudeau had made a point to learn everything he could about one of them, Wilbur Lyle, since the Pennsylvania native had arrived at Chinco. The young man's rating was Aviation Machinist's Mate, 2nd Class, and he was the designated plane captain. This made him absolutely essential to the success of the *Damnyankee* and her crew, as it was his job to keep the airplane in the air, from a mechanical standpoint. He knew every nut, bolt and rivet holding her together, or at least better pretend to, Trudeau knew! Lyle was responsible for making sure she was ready to fly, and would be depended upon to tell Trudeau if she wasn't---and why not. Lyle had been around the PB4Y-1's for several months now, having gone to aviation mechanics school in Memphis. He'd been assigned to the *Damnyankee* crew just recently. Six feet two, lanky, well-tanned with a face as open as the sun, he had a high school sweetheart back home. While a bit shy, he seemed to be a great guy, and the rest of the crew genuinely liked him. In fact, Trudeau thought, Lyle's ability to get along well with everyone was contributing to the fact that the group was becoming a family as well as a crew.

Lyle was excited about finally getting into the game at last, he'd admitted to Trudeau, after seemingly endless months of training and more training. He was excited about seeing another part of the world, and also about getting a shot at the Jerrys or the Japs, whichever it might be.

"Hey Skipper, rise and shine," Snavely said, with a gentle tug on Trudeau's flight vest. "The emergency just landed and everything is A-Okay. I thought we'd better get ready, as we're coming up next."

The pilot sat up in his seat, stretched his arms a bit, let out a groan, and with a quick shake of his head was focused once more. Trudeau was fast becoming a legend amongst his crew for his ability to grab a moment of sleep whenever it presented itself. While the pilot had no way of knowing this, his crewmembers took this as a sign that he was operating with an air of supreme confidence, and they liked that in their skipper.

"Wilbur, you happy with everything? Ready to go?"

"Aye aye, Skipper. Everything appears shipshape," sounded the response from over Trudeau's shoulder.

Wilbur fired up the putt-putt, the single cylinder gasoline engine that provided battery boost. The inboard starboard engine soon snapped, sputtered, and slowly metamorphosed from an initially noisy clatter to an increasing crescendo of brute power. As it came on line, smoothing out once it began to warm a bit, this single engine provided the generators with power to start the other three engines.

Trudeau felt a shiver work its way down his spine when the throaty Pratt and Whitney R-1830 Wasp engines came to life. Sporting fourteen radial, air-cooled cylinders, each of the P&W's put out 1,200 horsepower. Once all four of them were up and purring, the plane felt like the very description of power itself. Trudeau remembered the first time he'd ever experienced this in the cockpit of the big patrol bomber, and it had been both humbling and exhilarating.

He was heavily focused now as they began the power run up, where they analyzed the performance of all four of these huge power plants for magneto performance, oil pressure, engine temp, and so forth.

"OK fellas, this'll be our first test flight in our new home in the heavens, so let's get crackin' and make it a good one!"

The cockpit litany began:

"Booster pumps."

"On."

"Mixture."

"Auto rich."

"Props."

"Full high."

"Superchargers."

"Set."

"Half flaps."

"Set."

As Snavely and Trudeau advanced the throttles with brakes locked hard, the aircraft began to shake and rattle with increasing furor. Upon releasing the brakes, the big patrol bomber started to rumble and lurch down the runway, clumsily at first, then gaining grace and stability as she rushed down the tarmac, picking up speed as the great engines howled, then lifting off gracefully on her maiden voyage with her new crew.

While the flight was relatively brief---only three hours long---as they taxied back down the strip after returning to the base at Norfolk, the crew, to a man, felt excited at finally getting their own bird. The flight served Trudeau well as a baseline to see where they might improve operational and team skills over the next month of training. Overall, he was pleased with the initial effort, as both plane and crew performed credibly together.

Trudeau was well aware of the reputation of the PB4Y-1 for being difficult to fly, particularly at lower speeds, and he fully intended to explore every flight possibility and ramification over the next month of training before they left for combat duty. The steering yoke was huge, by aircraft standards, and it was work to keep the plane in trim, constantly having to wrestle it through the skies. Among Navy pilots, the joke was, a person could always tell an experienced Liberator pilot by his oversized left forearm.

Trudeau had one concern following a short discussion with his fellow officers; their relationship with the squadron training liaison officer, whom Snavely had nicknamed "Old Booger." For some reason the guy seemed antagonistic, and had been anything but helpful as the crew began their preparation for war. The incident with the keys was only one of a string of situations that were proving irritating, and in Trudeau's mind, unnecessarily so. Although Trudeau felt things were going well, he was continually irritated by the attitude of this one ground officer. Little stuff was proving a pain in the ass, like a malfunction of an oil-pressure gauge on the portside inboard engine, with the ground officer continually arguing and second-guessing them. He thought the sooner they left Norfolk the better. Overall, he was pleased with the progress of the crew.

CHAPTER VII

HAMMERING A FLIGHT CREW INTO A TEAM

The next month consisted of endless training flights, classroom sessions, and convoy escorts. The crew practiced navigation, wind drifts, bomb runs, and general gunnery at aerial targets. While there was still plenty of off-hour banter, Trudeau sensed a new level of seriousness as the crew realized that, while they seemed to be "playing war" at the moment, they were training for the real thing, and each day became more real as the training intensified.

Except for Joseph Edward Vigeant II, his new bow gunner, Trudeau had found precious little opportunity to learn a lot about the other men, but Vigeant stood out like the bass drum in a high school band. Brash and inquisitive, he demonstrated all the verve and wisecracking demeanor of a grizzled veteran, yet he was obviously among the youngest in the crew.

"You've got quite a name. What do we call you?" Trudeau had asked, upon their first meeting.

"Just call me Eddie, sir."

"How in the devil did you get into the Navy?"

Without the slightest hesitation, "I lied about my age, sir," Vigeant said.

"I'll bet you did," Trudeau responded. "How old are you now?"

"Nineteen."

"Dammit, Eddie, don't lie to me."

"Nosir," Vigeant said. "Eighteen."

Trudeau shook his head. "I might believe seventeen, but I'd be shocked if you were a day over sixteen."

Vigeant saluted. "Sir!" was all he said. Records would peg him at eighteen; he was the youngest of the *Damnyankee* crew.

J. Edward Vigeant grew up in the small town of Wynantskill, just outside of Hudson, along its namesake river in New York State. He was seven when his parents divorced, leaving him without a father. Although he despised school, he managed to get his high school diploma; while doing so, he played with the Hudson Boy's Club Band, and passionately built model airplanes.

His world, defined by his mother and his grandparents, was built around his dream of being able to fly some day. One distinction Eddie had was the fact that his grandfather had served as family physician at the Franklin Delano Roosevelt estate on the east bank of the Hudson, at Hyde Park. Beyond that, Eddie was just an everyday kid.

Having found his world revolving increasingly around the war, Vigeant had looked in his bathroom mirror anxiously for the last three days. With at least half an hour of aggressive massage each day, those little specks on his face that would have to serve as whiskers looked a bit more prominent, he thought. He was satisfied--- they added at least a year, he thought, which would bring him up to seventeen, and that should do the trick.

A little later on the third day of checking out his whisker condition, meager as it was, Eddie ran down the stairs and joined four of his pals, determined to do battle with either Japs or Nazis, or maybe both, as long as it was in an airplane. Eddie fell in with his chums as they headed off for the recruiting station in nearby Troy, where Vigeant and his pals offered themselves up to the United States Navy.

"Hey pal, you're first. Name?"

"Eddie," and he instantly felt it may have sounded too young.

"You got another name?"

"Okay, Yeah. Joseph."

"Okay, Eddie Joseph."

"No, Vigeant."

"Whatta you, a wiseass?"

"Nosir, my full name is Joseph Edward Vigeant, but I go by Eddie Vigeant."

"Don't call me 'Sir,' Joseph Edward Vigeant. You can save that for the officers."

"Sorry, what do I call you?"

"Who the hell cares. Call me Sam if you'd like, 'cause we ain't ever gonna see each other again. How old, kid?"

"Eighteen."

"You sure?"

"Yup."

"How long you been eighteen?"

"Seems forever, sir."

"I'll bet. Go on over there and fill out those papers."

"Okay, but I've gotta get into airplanes."

"Just fill that in where it says 'preferences.'"

The recruiting chief turned away from Vigeant and muttered to his yeoman. "Shit, sixteen if we give him a year. Sign him up. Maybe Mommy will come and grab him before we do."

Thus arrived, in due time, the baby of Trudeau's crew, but he was anything but. He had already served briefly in a PV-2 squadron in Brazil and showed himself to be a mover and a shaker. Vigeant might have been the youngest guy in the crew, but it didn't take long for Trudeau to make Vigeant his bow gunner.

According to scuttlebutt among the rest of the crew and overheard by Trudeau, women thought Vigeant was something special, and Trudeau could understand why. For such a young guy, Eddie had an aura of self-assuredness that belied his youth, and made him fun to be around.

He was smart, too. Despite his youth, he was also a natural leader, as Trudeau observed quickly. When it came time for liberty, it was Vigeant who did the talking and the scheming, and the rest listened. In the roughhousing that passed for recreation, it was Vigeant who often as not, came out on top. He was big, strong, and as the girls around the base noticed, he looked like an All-American boy on a Norman Rockwell *Saturday Evening Post* cover.

On that first day Trudeau had assembled his crew, he asked, "Is there anyone here who doesn't know how to swim?" and went down the roster.

"Lyle."

"Yessir."

"Beckwith."

"Yessir."

"Vigeant."

Like a fish, sir."

"Peterson."

"Yup. I mean yessir."

"Fleucher."

"Yessir."

Then a single hand rose. Cicero, another street-smart kid---but now his mouth was working, with nothing coming out.

Frank Cicero was a young Italian kid who had been born in New York, although he joined the service as a Chicago resident. He definitely had an urban edge. Cicero was a good-looking youngster, and Trudeau thought he probably did okay with the ladies, too. Trudeau peered at him intently. "You can't swim." It was a statement, not a question. No answer.

"Cicero, if you can't swim, what the hell are you doing in this man's Navy? How did you get past the phys-ed boys?" Trudeau wagged his head in mock disgust. "We spend our lives over water in this business. I'll have to teach you, I suppose."

Cicero brightened at this. "You were a lifeguard, sir."

"Who told you that?"

"The grapevine, sir."

"What else did the grapevine tell you?"

"It would make you blush, sir."

"Dismissed!"

Then to all of them he said, "Muster here at 0600 hours tomorrow. We'll be flying with an instructor. Familiarization for you, flying lessons for Mr. Snavely and me. Be on time. Satisfied with your quarters?"

"The Ritz."

"POW stuff."

"Knock it off. 0600. Be on time."

Thus Trudeau was learning about his officers and some of the enlisted crew, Lyle, Vigeant, and Cicero. He'd get to know all of them---Flecker, Fleucher, Peterson and Beckwith, too---along the way. With Cicero, though, he'd have to do better than that. In the little time he could scrounge, he'd teach him to at least tread water.

In Norfolk, memories of those first few days of flying at Chincoteague remained with Trudeau as he trained his new crew. He remembered the pang, the resentment at being a student once more, and knew how that rubbed raw against the eagerness to be combat-ready. After 18 months of teaching others how to handle the big flying boats at Pensacola, there he was back in the right seat again, the co-pilot's seat of the PB4Y-1.

He thinks back to an incident when the skipper's seat was filled with a grizzled veteran of the Pacific war, a raw-boned commander with piercing blue eyes. He was brusque, profane, all business.

"Airspeed in the empty bird 87 knots approx for liftoff."

The commander amputated words of over three syllables anytime he could. "Approx" meant approximately, exactly came back "xact," "accelerate" was "celrate," all, at least as far as his students could figure, to save precious time. Trudeau put in about an hour of "look-see" time before the commander spit out "takeoff." "Lander" following a single circuit of the island.

"You fly these before?" he asked.

"Nosir."

"PBY's? Flying boats?"

"Yes."

"Thought so. You have a tendency to land nose up a bit. I don't think you want to full stall your landing. You've got a tricycle landing gear here. Bring her in flat."

Trudeau brought her in flat for the next five circuits, then came the check. The commander pointed to the left-hand seat.

"You've got it. Take 'er off." He then folded his arms and pushed himself back into his seat. Trudeau had begun the long, rumbling takeoff run by shoving the throttles smoothly ahead, the commander quickly backing him up with his own hands to keep the throttles full on. Then the staccato rhythm of three gigantic tires beating against concrete runway plates grew, and Trudeau shifted both hands to the yoke to drive the plane down the mile-long runway. Soon she lifted off, gently feeling her way into the warm air, up two hundred, two-fifty, five hundred, and out over the marsh.

"What the hell!"

The plane took a lightning-quick, precipitous, sickening, nose-plunging, twisting bank to the left. Instinctively Trudeau made a quick roll to the right, wing down, nose down to pick up speed.

"Hang on. Hang on!" the commander shouted. He was grinning broadly. "You got 'er. Keep your bank to starboard."

The check. It was the-check-of-checks in a PB4Y-1---number one throttle yanked, port outboard engine suddenly dead, left wing dropping with reduced airflow from the prop, roaring starboard engines trying to shove you to the bad side. A load shift back to the right had to be swift; otherwise the result could be a catastrophic, spinning descent. Heavy planes like the PB-Y were slow to forgive, demanding quick reflex action.

"Okay, let's start 'er up again."

Trudeau worked the throttle and number one sputtered and farted and limped back to life, and the commander said, "Take 'er home."

Although Trudeau knew he had performed correctly, anger was welling up in him about the possible dire consequences of such an exercise.

He confronted the commander at the O-Club Bar that evening. "It was quite a test," he asserted, as calmly as he could.

"Forget it. You did fine. You can take your boys up alone tomorrow."

"I'm glad to hear that. Thank you. I'm glad I still *have* all my boys."

"Whaddya mean?"

"Isn't it kind of risky taking a full crew on that kind of maneuver?"

The commander eyed him carefully through flinty blue eyes. "I know what you mean." He looked passively into the bar mirror and the neatly placed regiments of scotch, bourbon and rye bottles lined up in column. "Your crew's gotta get used to emergencies too. When you get a chance, you may want to watch their reactions. That check was for them too. Bone 'em up for a kick in the ass like that. Where you're goin', everybody---*every*body---better act instinctively. Train their asses off, sonny. But don't try it on that young ensign," he added, meaning Snavely. "He won't be ready for awhile."

That was one day of training they would all remember. And one other experience would stand out, too, when they were coming in from the last night training flights over the Atlantic. Up front in the distance, a tiny, wavering light began to grow, and soon evolved into flames pushing and licking against the darkened sky. As they let down over a large patch of scrub pine forest on their approach to the runway, the blaze below became a long, flaming road like slash. They caught sight of a fuselage, or a piece of a fuselage, then they ghosted through a blanket of smoke before they touched down. As soon as they had rolled to a stop and shut down, one of the crew shouted at the signalman who had guided them to a parking strip.

"Who is it?"

"Rehor," came the reply.

Buzzie Rehor, Trudeau's bunkmate, a short, stocky redhead, good flier, everybody said.

"Aren't McKenzie and Sholinsky in his crew?" It sounded like Cicero's voice.

"Not anymore," somebody else said.

Off the plane, Snavely could be heard talking as he walked to the briefing room with some of the crewmen.

"Better get used to it. Be on your toes every minute."

Silence, occasionally ruptured by the wail of sirens, and the popping and crackling of the pines in the forest. This wasn't in the syllabus for neophyte warriors.

That night Trudeau's dreams were vivid. He dreamt of his bunkmate Buzzie. He dreamt of the crazy-assed Commander who cavalierly shut down his portside outboard engine when he was barely 1,000 feet off the ground. He dreamt of his young crewmembers.

Airman Second Class Joe Fleucher was a quiet kid, and Trudeau's first radioman. In the air, he occupied a small space on the starboard side of the aircraft, just behind and slightly below the copilot. He operated at a cramped little desk, where he could watch his transformer, receiver and transmitter, all of which were mounted above the desk. Fleucher was a handsome kid, a nice enough young man, not as outgoing as some of his crewmates, a little reticent to mix it up quite as much as some of the others.

Vernon Peterson was a tall, slim Airman Third Class, and the crew's second mechanic. A little older than some of the guys, Vernon was a well-mannered chap. Dependable was written all over his face.

Jerry Flecker was an Airman Third Class from Brooklyn who ran the portside waist gun. Flecker knew his way around, and knew how to handle himself. He had a New York City swagger, and Trudeau thought it might just serve Flecker well when they went to war.

Henry Beckwith came from Rhode Island. A tall, gangly kid, Henry was the second youngest in the crew, and at just 19 years of age, younger than everyone except for Vigeant, manned the starboard machine gun.

Trudeau tossed and turned in his sleep as the faces of his crew, intermingled with that of Buzzie, kept tumbling through his mind. He awakened in the morning, still feeling exhausted.

In less than a week, following the loss of Buzzie Rehor and his crew, they were on their way to another station, NAS Key West, Florida.

CHAPTER VIII

KEY WEST: ONE STEP CLOSER TO THE WAR

Mills hitched a hop on a Navy DC-3 to Chicago to see his wife. With Trudeau in the back seat, Carl and Helen Snavely cruised down Florida's Route 95 in their convertible, top down the entire trip from Chinco.

The enlisted crew went the hard way, by train, windows open to exchange the stifling air inside for the smoke, ash and embers from outside. Without any hassle from the Shore Patrol assigned to the train, they stripped to the waists and sat there glistening with sweat, moaning and griping.

"Kee-ripe, you know that damned Trudeau and Snavely went down to the Keys in a convertible?" Peterson sat upright. "Why in hell didn't I try for a commish?"

"You're stupid, that's why," Cicero charged.

The others chimed in, one by one.

"We're all stupid."

"Nah, just good luck and good breeding."

"Money."

"Education---you gotta have college to get in officer training."

Vigeant shook his head in disbelief. "You think all these guys are rich and lucky? We're still in a depression. Most of 'em probably worked their asses off to get to college. You had a chance."

Lyle was grinning as usual. He looked at Vigeant like a big brother.

"How did you learn so much in such a short time, Eddie?" Lyle asked, placing a calming hand on the junior crewman's shoulder. "You're right though, if we ever get out of this, we'll get our chance. Uncle Sammy will send us all off to be brain surgeons. A guy in the Legion told my folks the government will be paying for college."

Fleucher looked doubtful.

"Don't bet on it. Politicians. They tell you anything you want to hear to get elected."

Beckwith looked out the window, jerking his head back as a smoking black chip clipped the top of the window panel. "We could get killed right here. Maybe we better wait until it's over. It's a long way to Tipperary."

"Where'd you get that?" Peterson asked.

"My old man used to sing it. Came back from World War I. Here we go again!"

Key West had but one subject to teach them: how to attack submarines---lots of ways to attack submarines. For one thing, thanks to the Brits, the Allies now had radar. While radar couldn't see subs under water, it could sure as hell catch them on the surface. They learned to use the radar, and dropped smoke bombs on wood targets towed by either barges or a Navy sub. One day their smoke bombs were so far off target that they hit the towing sub.

In the age-old tradition of the Navy, the captain of the ship is responsible for whatever might go wrong. Despite his pleas that this was all a mistake, Trudeau was royally chewed out and sentenced to spend an afternoon in a towing sub, while smoke bombs were deliberately dropped on it.

Trudeau reported to his crew later, "The noise was deafening, so let's not do it again. Those poor guys down there!"

"How come they can't make soft smoke bombs so we can practice on the real thing," Cicero asked. "We proved we can do it!"

Beckwith looked at him with disbelief.

"You some kind of idiot? We were aiming at the tow target, and we hit the sub. Some marksmen!"

The next time around, their radio antenna dragged across the outer hull of the sub, creating another deafening racket, according to the sub crew, "worse than the roar of Niagara Falls." Trudeau was warned that additional infractions would land on his fitness report and could affect future promotion.

"Gentlemen, right about now we are stinking up the entire anti-submarine tactical school at Key West. At the moment, I must appear to be the dumbest goddamned pilot in the entire U.S. of A. Navy! First we hit the friggin' towing sub with a smoke bomb, and then...then, gentlemen...we drag our antenna right across the hull of a sub. We're gonna get better, and we're gonna get better awfully goddamned quick! Does anybody have anything to say?"

The crew was silent to a man, all studying something of intense interest in the area of their shoelaces. Trudeau was a hell of a good skipper, and to a man, they were deciding that whatever happened, they were going to tighten things up.

There were no more infractions, and they went on to the most demanding phase of the syllabus; conducting sneak attacks on surfaced subs. That meant night attacks: subs had to surface to replenish oxygen for both the crews and the batteries, and most of them did it under cover of night to avoid detection. Once on the surface, radar could pick them up.

The Navy's classified sub hunting equipment included a gigantic searchlight mounted on the underside of the starboard wing of the PB4Y-1. Once Trudeau and his boys learned how to properly employ the huge light, they swallowed hard and began what was clearly the most severe test of their mettle thus far.

Night after night they made radar sweeps over the Gulf of Mexico, picking up a Navy target sub. At 12,000 feet, they throttled back as they honed in on it, then dove to 2,000 feet altitude. They turned on the massive searchlight to blind the sub's gun crew, and hit it with a hailstorm of mock tracers and dummy depth charges---all in less than five minutes. Thus was their combat role ordained; this is what they would be doing once they got to England.

They learned one other thing at Key West---toughness. When yet another PB4Y-1 crew was lost in training, they discussed what might have gone wrong, in a somewhat businesslike fashion. They went on to the next challenge, and that was that.

By the time they departed for their last stateside temporary duty station at Norfolk---where they would at last receive their own plane ---they had begun to deal with the fact that they would need a certain amount of luck if they were to be able to survive their upcoming assignment in Europe.

CHAPTER IX

ENROUTE TO THE WAR IN EUROPE

After weeks of breaking the *Damnyankee* in, of countless navigation flights in and out of Norfolk along multi-angled practice routes, they finally received their orders to ship out on Wednesday, September 6, 1944, to the Navy base at Dunkeswell, England. Normally during the winter months, Navy Operations directed flights to Dunkeswell along a southern route, as it involved shorter over-the-water legs. Had the *Damnyankee* been issued orders to follow that route, they would have first headed south to Miami from Norfolk, then on to Brazil on the second leg, and eastward to the Azores, on the African coast, then north to the British Isles. Instead, because it was still early autumn, they received orders for the northern route, which would take them to New Hampshire, Labrador and Iceland.

At Dunkeswell, in Devon, they would be attached to Air Wing Five of the Twelfth Atlantic Fleet. Whatever, Trudeau thought. They just pay me to deliver this bird and the crew safely, and I guess they pick the destination and route. He settled himself into his cockpit seat and began once more to study the flight plan for the day and the pre-flight check list. Wow, he thought, here it is, we're finally getting the show on the road! I know now that my life is about to change irrevocably. Man, I'm trained, I got a great group of guys around me, and I'm ready!

Trudeau and his men had trained hard and well, and he felt a quiet satisfaction that the crew was solid, if not overly experienced. All of those countless hours of instruction and practice were going to be meaningful, once they were enroute to England and sure engagement with the Germans.

Trudeau turned to Mills. "Phil, the weather boys say we'll have contact all the way. Follow the iron compass and the Old Post Road to New Hampshire. You don't have any celestial on this, our first deployment leg, just surface. We're not going far, just a couple of hundred miles. If you want to try some wind drifts or shoot some sun lines, let me know. You don't have to be over water. It's probably a good idea to keep our nav as sharp as a tack.

"Wilbur, you there?" he then asked.

"Aye aye sir!" Lyle was on the flight deck, just behind Trudeau. During take off and landings, he would brace himself there, a third set of eyes to constantly observe and monitor the cockpit gauges, making sure that all four engines were functioning properly.

"Lieutenant, I went over the delivery report. The only thing they checked was the oil temp for number two. Nothing serious, but I'll keep my eye on it."

"Does it show in the run-up?"

"Doesn't say. Sometimes these things don't show when we rev the engines, but they will show up after we put a load on her, get her up in the air."

"Keep your eyeballs glued to those gauges."

"OK."

Trudeau had come to realize that "OK" was Wilbur's permanent response, no matter what you asked him to do. The word represented him. He'd found that out early on at Chinco when Wilbur demanded a tire change before he would sign off for a training flight. The crew chief had battled with a crusty Chief Petty Officer in charge of maintenance---and won. From that point forward, he was unquestionably the captain of the enlisted crew.

The *Damnyankee* lifted off the runway at Norfolk in routine fashion and on time, putting the wheels in the well just a moment or two past noon. Trudeau and the crew settled in for what promised to be an uneventful flight, with a touchdown at Grenier Field, New Hampshire estimated at 1730 hours.

Once over the Chesapeake Bay, Trudeau checked his compass heading with Mills and swung north. They would adhere to Army Air Transport Command routes from this stage forward. Goose Bay, Labrador, would be the real point of departure for the long overseas flight, and the spot where they would tie up any loose ends before tackling the long Atlantic crossing.

"Piece of cake," they all said in the British manner of the hop to New Hampshire. The trip, however, included a violation of altitude regulations enroute, one not unheard of among pilots. Over Bridgeport, Connecticut Trudeau nosed over, set his props roaring in low pitch and buzzed his own house---sending his wife indoors with their screaming, frightened baby girl.

"I'm glad your father didn't see that," he had said to Snavely.

"Hell, skipper, Dad would have loved it."

"You may be right. He's spent his career with guys who like to tear things up a bit. I enjoyed the dinner we had last night. Nice of your folks."

Snavely played with the propeller pitch controls.

"Little bit out of synch. She's still breaking in my ears. I'm glad you took 'em up on the dinner; I know you were busy with preps." He looked at Trudeau cautiously. "I didn't know how you might look at, uh, the situation. Did you think they were meddling?"

"Of course not. Just a couple of people who love their son. Pretty damned normal, if you ask me."

"Well, they're worriers. They wanted to meet you."

Carl Snavely, Sr. and his wife had decided to come to Norfolk to see their son off the night before, and had invited his skipper to have dinner with them. Trudeau had expected to be sized up by nervous parents, and was somewhat apprehensive. It made him feel like a camp counselor. He was also just on the edge of intimidation at the prospect of dining with someone famous, a man he had admired from afar through his own years as a football player. The renowned coach put him at ease immediately, and the evening had gone well despite his fears that the Snavely's might find him somehow lacking.

The *Damnyankee* landed at Grenier Field with no particular fanfare, and taxied over to a standby runway, next to a hangar. After a careful post-flight check, Wilbur Lyle noticed a small oil leak in the portside inboard engine (number two engine) oil cooler. He commandeered an entire Army Air Corps maintenance crew and marched it to the *Damnyankee* to fix the leak. Like a mother hen, Wilbur watched their work with a critical eye. They didn't skimp. And Trudeau watched Lyle, watching them. More than ever he became convinced that his luck was holding; Wilbur was a rare bird indeed.

As the crew began to walk across the tarmac after securing their plane, Vigeant turned to Cicero and said, "Hey Frankie boy, why do I feel that I'll probably shoot down four or five Jerries for each one you might accidentally wing? Do you think I'll just be that much better than you?"

Cicero winked at Flecker with a slight nod of the head and replied, "I dunno punk. Are you thinking that you might be able to *talk* them out of the sky? I was figuring on shooting mine."

Flecker laughed, and Vigeant just shrugged. It'd take a bit more than that to get him down.

Hearing the interchange, Trudeau realized duty was duty, and he was looking forward to watching this crew of his perform at the level he felt they would. He'd worked hard developing their skills, and felt they were a solid group, well matched with each other.

Snavely reminded his skipper of a matter he had brought up several times in the past---the tiny cockpit windows. Opened as wide as they could go, "only a midget in a bathing suit" could squeeze through them, Snavely claimed. A pilot of normal size wearing a heavy flight suit and a life vest---possibly inflated---would have quite a struggle, Trudeau agreed. Since weather was holding everyone tight to the base, the time was ripe for getting that worry out of the way. The windows could be opened much further if the "pinch" in the channels, which blocked the movement of the panes, could be opened up and set further back. Simple. With the help of some co-conspirators---Mills, Lyle and Peterson---the two pilots borrowed a hammer, a screwdriver and a portable ladder and did the job in half an hour.

"Carl, I fully agree with you that it could be a problem, and I'm glad we were able to find a way to fix it. Maybe we should both go to work as engineers at Consolidated when the war is over. You feel better?" Trudeau asked Snavely, who had satisfaction smeared all over his face.

"Yo, boss."

Trudeau eyed his crew. "Don't you guys mention this to anyone. You hear? Unauthorized alterations to Navy property can get us all tossed in the brig, or me, at least." His men nodded with gravity.

"C'mon, let's see what God-awful creation the Grenier chefs were able to cook up for dinner today," Trudeau said. Both Trudeau and Snavely headed across the hangar deck to hook up with Mills at the officer's mess, get a bite to eat, and go over the next day's training schedule.

The following morning machinist mate Lyle entered the squad bay door.

"Skipper, I think we've got a problem."

Trudeau looked up from a Navy publication he was reviewing, to see the lanky frame of Lyle backlit by the sun streaming through the door frame in the ready room.

"Come on in Wilbur. Tell me, what's the problem?"

Lyle entered, and without taking a seat, informed Trudeau that the fittings on the *Damnyankee's* oxygen tanks were not compatible with the connections on their oxygen masks.

"How might this have happened?"

Lyle explained, "Well Skipper, there might be just be that much difference between the Navy and Army versions of the aircraft. That's all I can figure. I spoke with their Av quartermaster, and he said we'd be lucky if we could get replacements in under seven to ten days. Probably have to get 'em all the way up here from the west coast. I do know that I can't jury-rig 'em. I already took a whack at it on one of them, but they're just too different."

"Well, Wilbur, how do you feel this will affect our hop to Goose Bay?"

"Skipper, I don't think you normally fly above ox level, do you?"

"No, you're right, but I'd sure like to have them, just as insurance. Let me hook up with Mills and Snavely. You'll be around if we need to talk with you, won't you?"

"Aye-aye Skipper, I'm staying in the hangar, just checking a few things out, and making sure that everything else is shipshape."

Lyle headed out as Trudeau summoned Snavely and Mills. The three of them sat down in the rickety little office.

"Fellas, Wilbur came in and told me there's been a small monkey wrench thrown into our plans."

"What do you mean, Skipper?" Mills asked, shifting forward on his chair. "What's the scoop?"

Trudeau explained what he'd been told by Lyle.

"Skipper, why don't we go over to the hangar and check this out in person?"

"Snave, that's exactly what I planned on doing. I guess I wanted input from both of you about this. I know if Wilbur can't jury-rig something, nobody can."

As they started toward the hangar, both junior officers told Trudeau that, while they would rather have the gear operational, neither of them felt it was worthy of stopping the mission, calling for what was commonly called a "down."

After surveying the situation, all three officers decided that the problem was insufficient to warrant delaying their arrival in Dunkeswell for almost two weeks. With the oxygen and window problems faced, however expediently, the *Damnyankee* crew looked like it was handling whatever came at it.

They were to remain at Grenier for four days, with further briefing scheduled to cover weather, navigation, warship recognition and first aid. The briefings seemed endless. They spent most of their waking hours in everything from foreign exchange rates to aircraft and ship silhouettes, from the dangers of venereal disease to writing letters home. These guys had already undergone months of training, and while some of the information in the stuffy, sterile classroom was repetitious and dry, there was a freshened sense of mission that made the time at Grenier bearable. Warship recognition briefings in particular carried a new feeling of relevance, far different than the days back in Virginia. This time, these guys knew they were going off to fight in the war, and there isn't much else in a young man's life that can do a better job of getting his attention.

"Hey Jerry, whaddya think about our chances to pop a couple of German warships?" asked Eddie Vigeant, with a cigarette dangling from his lower lip, while he surveyed the cards in his hand.

"Well, country, I'd feel a lot better if we had a big city guy like me or Frankie up there in the bowgunner's turret. I'm not so sure a country guy like you could tell a cruiser from a Holstein cow."

Cicero chuckled, as he and Flecker loved to tease the younger Vigeant about his upstate New York roots. The three of them, along with Vernon Peterson, were playing cards on a sea chest in the transient enlisted barracks.

"Oh yeah, well here you go Frankie boy," said Vigeant, as he slapped his cards down, and said, "See if either of you two city boys can identify this!"

Eddie's hand showed a straight flush to the jack of spades. It was

Vigeant's turn to chuckle, as he saw the pain on both Flecker's and Cicero's faces. Cicero turned his cards over, revealing three kings and two fours. "Shee-it," said Flecker, as he contemptuously tossed his cards on the chest. His full house kings over fours wouldn't get the job done this time.

While the entire crew got along well, it divided somewhat naturally according to personalities. Vigeant, Cicero and Flecker were the wise guys, and tended to continually rag on each other, almost always without rancor. Joe Fleucher, Vernon Peterson, Wilbur Lyle and Henry Beckwith weren't quite as crazy as the other three, but by and large they all got along, and looked to cover each other's backsides.

Just before noon on their fifth day at Grenier Field, on Sunday, September 10, the *Damnyankee* raced down the runway between hills set ablaze with New England fall colors. They set course for Goose Bay, Labrador, some 840 miles to the northeast. Another piece of cake, they felt. After lift off and the increasingly familiar chore of getting the big white bird up to their designated altitude, Trudeau turned the controls over to Snavely for awhile, and sat back as well as he could in the pilot's seat, reflecting on the past few days.

After all the crew selection, training, retraining, and more training, he was finally going to war. He hadn't really considered leaving Rita and baby Rita behind in a rented flat in Pocomoke, Virginia. He felt they would be in much better hands back in Connecticut for the duration. Trudeau was happy that he had done exactly that. With all that he had on his plate, he knew they would be better off among family, and that he would feel more at ease to concentrate on his wartime duties.

He had hoped for an assignment in the South Pacific, as that seemed to be more "Navy" territory than the Atlantic. He assumed that they would be sub-hunting and going after some surface shipping in the Bay of Biscay, but it wasn't like the Army boys hadn't already been doing that.

Jim couldn't help but wonder how long it would be before he could be reunited with his girls. There had been war talk forever, it seemed, but the cold reality of it was beginning to seep into his consciousness, as they were already on the second leg of his journey to war. Well, he thought, he and the crew were well-prepared, and what else could they ask for? That and perhaps just a dollop of good luck.

So much had happened since he graduated from Ohio University just a year and a half before. He had been stationed in Pensacola, flying sea-based aircraft, and then was transferred up to Norfolk, to Chinco, Key West, and back to Norfolk. He thought about *Damnyankee,* too. The PB4Y-1, the Navy's version of the Consolidated Vultee-built B-24 Liberator bomber, was 66 feet long. Its non-fueled weight of over 15 tons and a wing span of 110 feet meant the PB4Y-1 was not a particularly easy plane to fly. Trudeau had learned from experience they were a handful at low speeds, and he had heard stories from other Liberator jocks of wing tip, and actual fuselage twists occurring on these aircraft after a particularly difficult flight.

He did feel comfortable with both Snavely and Mills, and was going to try to find some way to get Mills a little stick time, if possible. He knew the navigator gig was eating at the young Ensign, as all pilots want to fly, and not simply plot courses. He was a good stick, but at the same time, Trudeau knew that regs were regs.

It was nice to have a spanking new aircraft, and this bird's Bureau of Weapons (buweps) number 38799 showed the beginning of a pretty good poker hand, which he and his card-crazy crew took as a good omen. The men had also taken to *Damnyankee* as the name of the plane like a duck to water.

"Skipper," Snavely called over the mike, "Take a look at the weather ahead, will you?"

"Thanks, Snave. Phil, how are we looking with this front?"

"Skipper, it looks like everything is going to be pretty well socked in once we cross the St. Lawrence. We are getting good radio readings, and I think we will be fine if we continue at 7,000 feet."

"Thanks, Phil, good job," Trudeau replied.

The entire hop from Grenier to Goose Bay was about 840 nautical miles, and if all went well, they should be touching down just about 1800, right in time for a warm meal, compliments of the Navy chef.

The weather proved untroublesome. Just before closing down the bird on the Goose Bay tarmac, Mills did a quick calculation and told Trudeau, "Hey Skip, I just did a fuel eval, and she drank about 50 gallons per hour. Not bad for such a big bird."

"See Phil, that's what you get when you couple the best skipper and the best navigator in the entire goddamned U.S. Navy," Trudeau retorted over his shoulder as he swung down out of the bomb bay after landing.

Goose Bay looked like a most forlorn place. Following dinner at the mess, the crew gathered outside the transient enlisted quarters for an after-dinner smoke, including the three officers.

"Wow, Skipper" asked Airman Vigeant, "what would you have to do to piss someone off enough to have to stay at Goose Bay for the rest of the war?"

Trudeau looked around at the remoteness of the Goose Bay flight station, chuckled a bit, and said, "Eddie, Ensigns Mills, Snavely and I were just talking at mess about leaving one of our crew here. With your social skills, we thought you might best represent the crew of the *Damnyankee*."

"You know Lieutenant, I appreciate your confidence, but after thinking about it, I believe Jerry Flecker is your man. He is much better at the P.R. stuff than yours truly." Flecker, the street-wise kid from Brooklyn, caught Vigeant's eye just long enough to give him the one-finger salute.

"Lieutenant, I appreciate Airman Vigeant's suggestion, but I feel Labrador could do better with someone with a more rural background. You know something like a rube from upstate New York."

"Well guys, we've got a few days here to get ready before we head over the big pond. We'll spend a little more time on vessel recognition, and we'll check and re-check our gear. If the weather stays acceptable, we should be out of here in a couple of days. I don't know about you guys, but I'm going to take a little walk just to get the kinks out, and then I'll hit the rack. We'll be at it bright and early in the morning."

Trudeau field-stripped his butt, sprinkling the remainder over the ground, and began his walk. Man, he thought, if I have to go to war, I can't think of a better group of guys to do it with.

With the sun now sliding beneath the remote tundra of Labrador, Trudeau shivered a bit, and turned towards the transient officers quarters. Tomorrow would come soon enough, he thought.

In a few hours, they were back in the briefing room for more intensive instruction, including how little money they were allowed to take overseas. There followed that evening a great run on the base's abundance of slot machines waiting to swallow whatever the crewmembers were forced to pare from their wallets.

At Goose Bay, they inventoried ceaselessly, checking again and again their emergency gear, life vests, rubber dinghies, flares, Gibson Girl transmitters, shark repellant and where it was all stowed---just in case they went down.

Skylarking amongst the crew had all but disappeared now, the fun having been left behind. They were all weary of the endless trainings and briefings. Plus the place was incredibly gloomy, a seemingly endless stream of uniforms shuffling into white planes and olive drab planes incessantly heading off into the night. The very air around Goose Bay seemed charged with a strange mixture of both purpose and gloom. Old stuff to combat veterans, it was new to the untested crew of the *Damnyankee.* Without acknowledging it in so many words, they knew they were outward bound into an unknown world where the desire to survive ruled the minds of men.

The next few days dragged on, as the remoteness of Goose Bay, plus the anticipation of finally arriving in England and getting on with their version of the war, had the crew anxious for the next leg of the flight. This would be to Meeks Field, near Reykjavik, Iceland, for fuel; they would then go across the North Atlantic to Scotland for another fuel stop at Prestwick, south to England and the hookup with FAW-7 at Dunkeswell. They had hoped to be able to find replacement parts for either the oxygen tanks or their masks at Goose Bay, but no such luck. Trudeau would certainly have preferred having the oxygen aboard, but the flight to England could be concluded without ever having to go to oxygen level. He knew this wouldn't have been feasible for the Army version of the plane, the B-24, which was used as a high-altitude bomber in Europe, and needed to climb high enough to avoid anti-aircraft fire from the Germans, enroute to their bombing missions over Europe. The Navy's PB4Y-1 had a different mission, that of patrolling the ocean, and would normally be working at much lower altitudes.

Several scheduled departures for the *Damnyankee* were canceled, due to unfavorable weather reports. The crew filled in the time with more training exercises. The blasted delays were beginning to grind on the crew, and they got tired, quickly, of rising in the middle of the night for a briefing, only to have it cancelled due to weather. The grayness of the weather in Labrador could work on a man's psyche, they found.

Trudeau repeatedly emphasized checks on the life-saving gear, with nothing but long ocean flights ahead of them. It was all properly stacked and secured in the aft section of the PB4Y's fuselage, and set up for quick release, were the need to arise.

Trudeau had already decided that for the flight from Goose Bay onwards, he would require all crewmembers to wear their Mae West life jackets as a standard precaution. In the evenings, Trudeau would pop into the enlisted quarters to see how the guys were doing. There was usually a card game, but he began to notice a few of the crew sitting near their lockers, writing letters to home.

As he walked back out into the cool Labrador evening, he couldn't help but wonder what was in store for these guys. At 26, he was referred to as the "old man." Trudeau didn't mind that at all, but he couldn't stop thinking how young they all were, and how much he hoped he could keep them safe in the days and months ahead.

The reality of the hazards they might face came down hard in a briefing on Emergency Landing Fields, "sanctuaries from the sea," if they had to set down after passing the "PNR," the Point of No Return, when fuel capacity would be diminished too much to allow getting back to the point of origin. One of these Emergency Landing Fields was at the southernmost tip of Greenland, "Bluie West One." Although hundreds of aircraft had gone in and out of BW1 successfully, its spectral appearance was little consolation to the untested. On the photograph projected on the screen, it resembled a long, dark tunnel, a glacier between mountains with a lead-solid ceiling of low hanging clouds. The tunnel forked, the right leg leading to a sloped emergency runway, the left into a mountain wall.

"It's usually very foggy," the briefing officer said. "Don't make a mistake."

"I'd rather ditch," an Army pilot shouted.

"No you wouldn't," came the rejoinder. "Hitting the mountain is quicker and cleaner."

Phil Mills reported the next day that he had dropped his octant, their sensitive navigation instrument, hard on a concrete floor. If it were damaged even slightly, any resulting error could be magnified enough to seriously throw off their position "fixes."

"Can't you have it re-calibrated here?" Trudeau asked. "Surely a base like this would have the means to do so, or an extra octant."

"No."

They had a replacement for the Army boys; the Navy would have to draw from their own stores.

Snavely looked at Trudeau. "You gotta call Old Booger," he said.

Lyle nodded, and spoke up. "There's something else," he said.

"I know, the oxygen. We're going without it."

"No sir, the electrically heated flight suits. They got the wrong plugs. They don't fit our receptacles. Maybe our plane is a new model, they changed things."

"Damn."

Trudeau headed for the base operations building to call Old Booger back in Norfolk, who, as anticipated, was unsympathetic.

"Trudeau? TRUDEAU! What in hell…"

"Keep your shirt on, sir. We got problems."

"What else? What's the matter with you guys?" he demanded angrily. "You seem to be doing everything possible to abort."

"No one's trying to abort." Trudeau clenched his fists in anger. "You think we should go without ox, that's okay, but my navigator dropped his octant and our electric flight suits…"

"I don't want to hear it. You don't have the slightest idea of the conditions a lot of our boys are putting up with. Go. GO!" He hung up.

Trudeau resigned himself. All things considered---the time of the year and clearing weather---they should have no trouble at their assigned altitude. At that, they were lucky so far. He thought of other planes, other crews, the conditions they had to overcome to complete their missions---dead crewmen, crippled aircraft, foul weather. They would go.

Goose Bay was a dreary place, and within just a few days, all ten members of the *Damnyankee* crew were anxious to clear out of this godforsaken spot and get on to merry old England. Just one more leg to Iceland's Meeks Field for fuel, and then on to Europe to join the war.

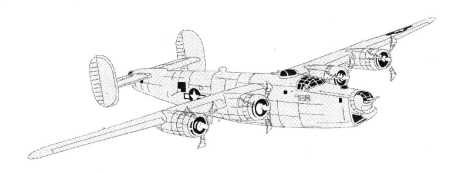

US Navy PB4Y-1

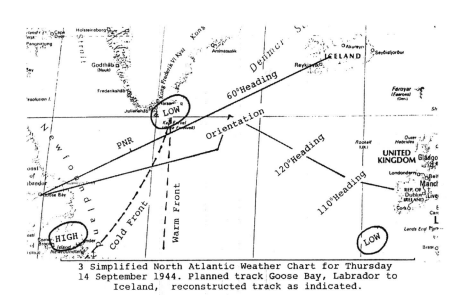

3 Simplified North Atlantic Weather Chart for Thursday
14 September 1944. Planned track Goose Bay, Labrador to
Iceland, reconstructed track as indicated.

North Atlantic weather graph on 9-14-44

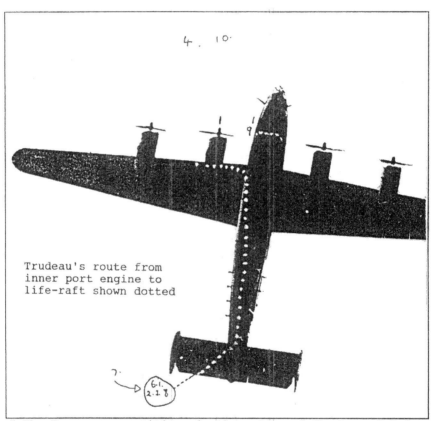

5 The Known crew positions in the water. 1-Trudeau, 2-Lyle,
3-Cicero, 4-Mills, 6-Vigeant, 7-Flecker, 8-Beckwith,
9-Snavley, 10-Peterson.

Silhouette of plane in water, with known crewmen positions;
number 5 was Fleucher (location unknown).

Damnyankee crew in dress whites, Norfolk, Virginia

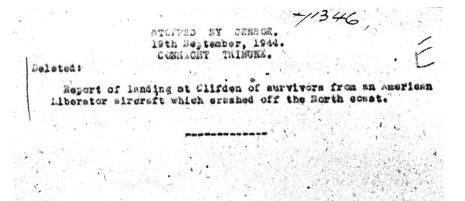

Censored report of American Liberator airplane ditching,
Connaught Tribune, Sept. 19, 1944

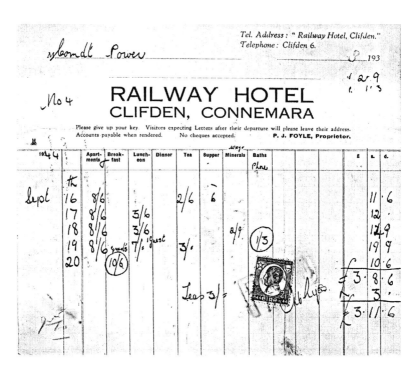

Lodging bill for Commandant Powers at Railway Hotel,
Clifden, Connemara

Irish cottage which first provided refuge to the
Damnyankee survivors.

District Hospital,
Clifden,
Co. Galway.

22. 9. 1944

Comdt. J. Power,
Athlone

Dear Mr. Power,

I enclose the bill for the airmen and
you will notice 5/8 for phone calls.
I have paid that so you can send me
cash separate from the official account.
I have added on 5/- for a call that
went on the Hospital a/c and when I
am sending on the money to Galway I
will mention that call.

Best wishes.

Yours sincerely,

Sr. Mercy.

[handwritten signature]

Phone bill to Commandant Powers from Sister Mercy at Clifden hospital

<u>C O P Y</u>

Particulars of telephone calls from Clifden District
Hospital which were booked as private calls
from P.O. Call Office

18. 9. 44 - 4. 55. p.m.   Ballymena   630911 -   2/10
18. 9. 44 - 4. 55 p.m.   Dublin   71981 -   2/10

                                        Total -   5/8

                              Certified
                                    P. Seoigheach.
          Clifden   Maistir Puist
             X
          22 sp .
            44
        CO. GALWAY

Typed copy of Irish Army phone calls from Clifden hospital,
submitted by Postmaster

The Ailleabreach harbor and wharf today.

The five survivors and Olive Hardy at Clifden Cottage Hospital, with
Trudeau in the foreground.

as follows:

James O Trudean
Wilbur D. Lyle (dated Sept. 18th 1944)
Gerald Fletcher (dated Sept. 18th 1944)
Frank P. Cicero
Joseph Edward Vigeant (dated Sept. 18th 1944)
I must have received all five
autographs on the same date as
the two undated ones are in between
pages dated Sept. 18th 1944.

This statement has been read over
to me and it is correct.

Signed.
Olive Harley
Witnessed: A. Kelly Sergt. 105ne.

Handwritten deposition from Olive Harley to Sean Kelly, confirming
the authenticity of her autograph book

Eddie Vigeant in leather crew jacket

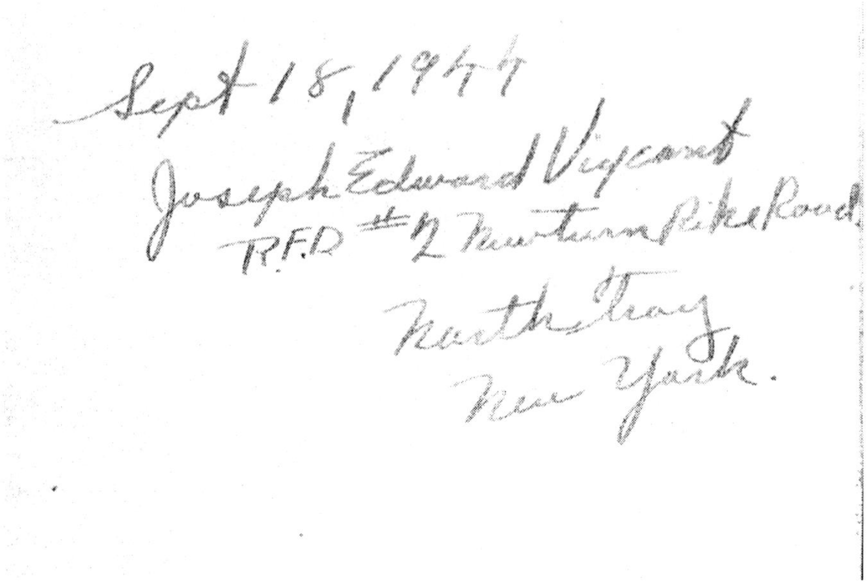

Sept 18, 1944

Joseph Edward Vigeant

R.F.D. #2 Newtown Pike Road

North Troy

New York.

Eddie Vigeant's autograph

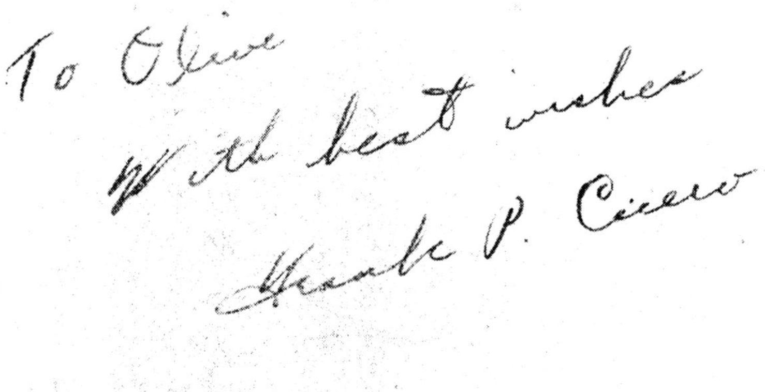

To Olive

With best wishes

Frank P. Cicero

Frank Cicero's autograph

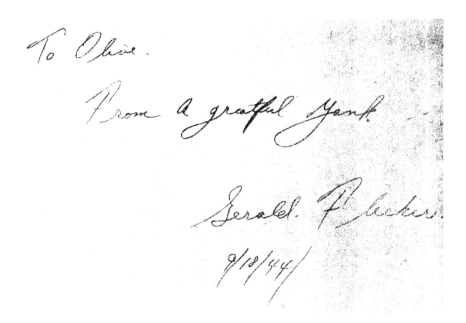

Jerry Flecker's autograph

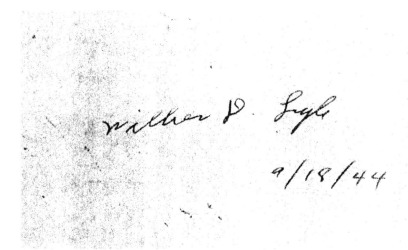

Wilbur Lyle's autograph

To Oline —
who carried hand in hand
with God and Ireland to
welcome us from the sea.

James O. Trudeau

Jim Trudeau's autograph

The *Damnyankee* monument.

G.2 French,
Western Command,
Castlebar Barracks.

(5) One Death Certificate supplied by Mrs. King,
Asst. Registrar and paid for by me (Comdt. Power) £-. 2. 7d

(6) Coffin with remains was held in Clifden
Protestant Church overnight on 16/9/44. Door of
Church opened at my request at 10.00 hours on the
following morning. Paid to Sexton by me
(Comdt. Power).................................... £-. 2. 6d

(7) A.F. 18 from Quartermaster, C.T. & M. Depot to
Comdt. Power in respect of one Singlet Gym -
Survivors were issued with underclothing on day
of removal. When clothing was withdrawn one
singlet was found to be missing.................. £-. 2. 9d

(8) Meals to Survivors at Imperial Hotel, Ballina

5 Dinners @ 4/- each   £1. 0. 0)
Refreshments   5. 0) £1. 5. 0d

(9) Dr. W.B. Casey, "Stella Maris", Clifden

Medical attendance on five Survivors from the
16/9/44 to 20/9/44. Visit to Allenbrach and
report on death of H. Beckwith to Civil
                                Authorities........ £25. 0. 0d

(10) James O'Malley, Allebrach, Ballyconneely, Clifden

This man distributed ½ pint of brandy to the
Survivors after they had been brought to Michael
Conneely's house.   £-. 14. 0d
I also recommend that this man be paid the sum of
£1 for services performed by him on the occasion. £1. -. 0d

(11) Michael Conneely, Allebrach, Ballyconneely, Clifden

It was to this man's house that the Pilot and Gunner called.
Conneely immediately aroused Martin O'Malley of Doonhill L.O.P.
who lives near him but in his haste omitted to tie his boots
properly and lost one of them which he was afterwards unable
to recover - Size 9. He also provided the Survivors with his
ration of tea and wrapped them in blankets and other available
clothing. Conneely is a man of about 55 years of age, unmarried,
and lives alone. I recommend that he be paid the sum of £5
which, in my opinion, would not be excessive.

(12) Ten (10) gallons of petrol and two (2) pints of oil supplied from
Castlebar Military Barracks to U.S. Vauxhall car No. GS-7722 -
drawn and signed for by me (Comdt. Power) at Castlebar.

                                    _____
                                            COMMANDANT
                                            (J. Power)

Commandant Powers' expense list, including Beckwith's coffin,
Jimmy O'Malley's whiskey, and Michael Conneely's lost boot

.INA

September ...194*4 4*

To *Imperial Hotel,* Dr.

(J. McMONAGLE, Proprietor).

Sept. 20				
11 Dinners @ 4/:		2	4	—
Liquors.		-	18	8
	£	3 - 2	8

2/)
2/6

Imperial Hotel bill for eleven dinners,
enroute to Northern Ireland 9-20-44

...an Barrett TD (left), Ms Patricia McKenna
...Mr Proinsias De Rossa TD. The ride was held to
...the city. Photograph: Jack McManus

...ced ...ool board n proposals

Dublin by the Irish National Teachers Organisation (INTO) and the National Parents Council — Primary (NPC).

"Even our teachers, at times, can be reluctant to accept the responsibility and effort of management," she said. "The serious engagement in management derives from the fact that the board of management is — and must be seen to be — the management authority in the school."

She added that the "focus for action" would move away from the clerical chairperson of the board to the board as a group.

She suggested the promotion of the school or parent-teacher ciations, without managerial onsibility, as a means of pro- g valuable support services ools.

nts had a vital role to play orting teachers, especially as of pupils' self-esteem, and the needs of children with disability, the general of the INTO, Senator , told the conference. le called for a tre- ources, places and special education, was "appallingly ". He also sug- aching of entre- uld begin at

io has gained nic ability in ects through third-level too inhib- n on the rch and er 20s." e 17

'y for ools po- ire nt t-

US pilot recalls wartime rescue in Connemara

By Alan Harman and Audrey Magee

A VETERAN United States pilot this weekend relived the night 50 years ago when he almost died many times over on a hostile Co Galway coast and the second World War touched the people of a small Connemara community.

Lieut James Trudeau, now 77 and living in Gainsville, Florida, walked the beach at Ballyconneely and remembered that in the space of 36 hours in September 1944 he survived a plane crash, a hostile Atlantic storm and the deadly embrace of hypothermia before being thrown up on the beach.

By the time local residents found his crew, one of his companions had died, but four others, although unconscious, had survived.

This weekend Lieut Trudeau unveiled a plaque commemorating the dramatic events of five decades ago. Then a pilot in the US navy, he was ferrying a B-24 bomber from Norfolk, Virginia, to Dunkeswell, England.

His route included fuelling stops in Goose Bay, Canada, and Iceland, but the aircraft was blown off course and missed Iceland. With the wings iced up and the aircraft out of fuel, Lieut Trudeau had to ditch in hostile seas.

Six of the 10-man crew scrambled into a life raft and fought for survival, capsizing three times before they were washed ashore.

A secret report at the time

sent to the chief staff officer of G2 branch of the Department of Defence said it was thought the aircraft had crashed in the region of Blacksod.

Lieut Trudeau struggled a quarter of a mile inland and made his way to the only light in the darkness, the home of the late Michael Conneely, a fisherman then aged 55. Conneely alerted James and Martin O'Malley, who were joined by a third brother, Mark, and after a frantic search they found the beached life raft.

The men were carried to Conneely's house where they were brought back from the brink of death with the help of a handy half-pint bottle of whiskey. They were then moved to the Clifden District Hospital where they recovered from their ordeal.

On Saturday night Lieut Trudeau met the surviving rescuers of 50 years ago and yesterday afternoon, watched by almost 150 people, a plaque was unveiled by him and Mrs Dorothy Vigeant at Aillebrach, near the site of the rescue. Mrs Vigeant, from Troy, New York, is the widow of another member of the crew, Edward Vigeant, who died about 18 months ago.

The only other surviving member of the bomber crew is Mr Gerald Flacker of New York City, who was unable to travel to Ireland for the weekend events.

Trudeau's Irish Times interview at monument dedication, 9-12-94

4907 Calvert St.

Cincinnati 9, New York

Nov. 28, 1944

Mrs. J. Trudeau

Bridgeport Conn.

Dear Mrs. Trudeau,

I have learned through Mr. C. G. Snavely that your husband, Lt. James Trudeau went through Cincinnati, but was unable to locate me, which I regret very much. If I were away at the time, I am so very sorry to have missed his visit, for I would have been eager to learn more about the plane crash in which my son, Vernon Petersen, was lost.

I am Vernon's mother, and of course am anxious to know all about the fate of my son. I grieve so much to know he is among the four missing men of the crew, who were from all appearances, swept away by the waves. It does look hopeless to us that their lives should have been spared, yet it is only natural to cling to a faint ray of hope and to keep praying that the Lord somehow may have spared them.

I rejoice with you that your husband's life was spared. Often Vern spoke of how much he thought of his pilot and how he admired his steady ability, and his hesitancy to take chances.

To have been lost in actual battle would have been terrible enough; but this needless tragedy, caused by Navy negligence makes our grief even worse, if possible. I hope that Mr. Snavely's letter to high Naval authorities will prevent further tragedies of this sort.

I deeply appreciate Lt. Trudeau's trying to find me and am so sorry he was unable to do so. If you can give me any further information at any time as to the fate of my son, Vernon, I would be very grateful to you.

May the Lord protect your husband from harm and return him safely to you again. With best wishes and the Lord's blessing, Sincerely,

Ruth Peter.

Letter from Vernon Peterson's mother to Mrs. Trudeau; 11-28-44

Lt. James O. Trudeau
USNR (V)
74 MacArthur Avenue
Closter, New Jersey

Dear Lt. Trudeau:

Your letter of 26 September with attached synopsis, addressed to Dr. Nesbitt, is gratefully acknowledged. As the Project Officer of this Sea Survival Study, I find your detailed account most helpful, not only as a record of what occurred but of how you felt. Few of those to whom we have addressed similar letters for aid in this study have proved as articulate in this respect.

I am a Cornell graduate and a contemporary of Coach Snavely and his son Carl. This account of Carl Snavely's death is the first information I have had. For this reason I can add that your report makes interesting, but sad reading.

Our purpose in analyzing survival incidents is to learn from the experience of others. Your cooperation and splendid reports are an excellent contribution to this study.

Sincerely yours,

GEORGE A. LLANO
Research & Editorial Specialist
Arctic, Desert, Tropic Information
Center

Letter from George Llano, Research Studies Institute, Maxwell Air Force Base, to Jim Trudeau, 10-10-52

Kneeling foreground, left to right: Gerald Flecker, Frank Cicero, Vernon Peterson (lost at sea). Standing, left to right: Wilbur Lyle, J.G. Fleucher (lost at sea), Phillip Mills (lost at sea), James Trudeau, Carl Snavely (lost at sea), Henry Beckwith (drowned in dinghy), J. Edward Vigeant III

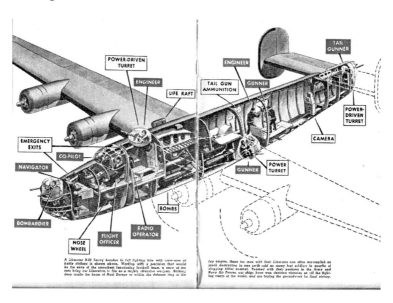

Cutaway of PB4Y-1 with crew members at station

Trudeau's Short Snorter, signed by Admiral John Hall Jr.

Jim Trudeau and Dorothy Vigeant at the dedication of the
Damnyankee memorial, 1994.

Sean and Maureen Kelly with the author.

CHAPTER X

TROUBLE IN THE AIR

Finally, at 0230 Greenwich Mean Time on Thursday, September 14th, 1944, they began the final flight briefing for the hop to Iceland and Meeks Field, securing the briefing two hours later.

The weather dope showed a 1020 millibar high south of Newfoundland and another 1028 millibar high directly south of Cape Race. There was a 1000 millibar low immediately south of Greenland with a cold front running back towards Newfoundland from this pressure system. Iceland had a heavy cloud cover with high pressures rising east of Iceland in the direction of the British Isles.

Trudeau had set a liftoff time of 0730 hours, but they encountered some difficulty in running up the portside outboard engine (number one), and by the time they got the balky Pratt and Whitney running smoothly on all 14 cylinders, and had the other three engines up and running, they had used up almost 100 gallons of AV fuel sitting on the runway. This shouldn't have any negative effect on the flight, though. At takeoff they carried 2,900 gallons for a 13-hour flight of about 2,300 miles.

"I wonder why that damned number one engine was so balky," Trudeau muttered to no one in particular.

"Skipper, sometimes they act like a fine horse and get a bit cantankerous. I wouldn't worry any if I were you," Lyle answered. "Everything on all the gauges looked fine, and she was purring like a big cat when we lifted off."

"Hey Snave, check out the stars," Trudeau said, as *Damnyankee* climbed into a clear sky. Morning was just breaking. Trudeau nudged the *Damnyankee* up to a cruising elevation of 7,000 feet, and corrected to 60 degrees magnetic, as called out by Ensign Mills.

"Hey Phil, we're finally out of that hell hole Goose Bay, and on to England," Trudeau said into the intercom.

"Roger, Skipper, and we didn't leave that place any too soon for me," Mills answered.

The entire crew breathed a collective sigh of relief, as this meant they were finally going to war, and they felt ready to a man.

"Eddie, what do I hear from you this morning?"

"Skipper, I'm ready and rarin' to go," came the reply. Vigeant's position, as bow gunner, took a special kind of guy. He had to be a contortionist just to take up position in the PB4Y-1, getting down almost on his hands and knees to slide himself into position through the nose wheel section of the aircraft. Unlike the B-17, the B-24, of which the PB4Y-1 was a naval conversion, used a tricycle landing gear, whereas the B-17 had the three-point tail wheel set-up. For a non-combat flight like this, there would be no need for Vigeant to shoehorn himself into the bow turret.

The cloud cover started to get heavy as the flight proceeded, and an occluded front east of Iceland ran back southerly towards Ireland. At the 7,000 foot flying level, the weather was clear and the stars shone like brilliant diamonds against the background of a dark blue sky. Visibility was estimated at 5 to 8 miles, so flying conditions were good.

Trudeau held the big ship steady on a course of 60 degrees magnetic, as supplied by navigator Mills. Along this course they would just nick the south coast of Cape Farewell in Greenland enroute to Iceland. At takeoff, all instruments were solid, as were all four of the big Pratt and Whitney's.

About two hours out of Goose Bay, Trudeau felt a tap on his right arm and turned around to see Airman Second Class Joe Fleucher at his elbow.

"What's up, Joe?"

"Skipper, I've been having a few problems with the radio. It's been breaking up on me, and lots of static. I shut her down for a minute, tested all the tubes to make sure they were solid, and I think things should work. I just wanted to let you know."

"Okay Joe. Stay on top of it and let me know if it keeps screwing up."

Trudeau didn't want to appear overly concerned, but in the back of his mind he did some calculations as to when they would reach the Point of No Return, and wanted to be sure his radio was working prior to that. It was now about 1000 hours, and he had a good one to two hours before decision time.

"Phil, be sure to keep us on course, and continue to take your wind drifts. I think we're fine, but if Fleucher encounters radio problems, I'll be depending on you even more than ever."

Mills nodded his assent, even as he was working out a dead reckoning position. In a matter of minutes the cloud cover broke a bit, and they were able to see the coast of Greenland. It was more white than green, through the smatterings of cloud. It looked as if they were fairly near Cape Farewell, which validated the job Mills was doing at the nav station.

Fleucher notified Trudeau about half an hour later that the radio appeared to be solid, and radioed for and received clearance for the flight to continue on its route towards Iceland. They were flying now above 70 percent cloud coverage, and around 1030 hours they encountered the anticipated warm front. Navigation continued via dead reckoning, and Mill's drifts were very consistent when they were checked against forecasted winds and drift. They approached the Point of No Return around noon. Mills completed two position fixes at the tiny nav deck, one with a sun line and track, and the other with sun line and no-wind plot. True headings were checked with the *Damnyankee's* astro compass.

Once again, though, the radio began incurring problems and interference, probably weather static. That kept Fleucher from getting any radio bearings to cross-check Mill's work.

The most recent fixes placed the *Damnyankee* about 100-150 miles south of their intended route. Trudeau, after consulting with both the navigator and co-pilot, changed course slightly. "Phil, if we alter course 20 degrees to portside, I believe we'll be able to hook onto the northwest beam of the Meeks Field radio beam. That should get us right back on track. What do you think?"

Mills agreed on this plan of action, and they both were relieved when Fleucher announced a few minutes later that he was pretty sure he had just picked up a radio beam from Meeks Field. Some more static again caused them to lose the beam.

By now they had hit the cold front, and along with it increasingly heavy interference, rendering the radio useless. Both Trudeau and Snavely now noticed ice build-up on the wings, due to the cold front. The thin Davis wings fitted on the PB4Y-1's were notorious for icing up, giving credence to a saying amongst the pilots, "the amount of ice you'd put into a drink would be sufficient to kill its lift." *Damnyankee* was beginning to experience first-hand the reality of that statement.

"Snave, let's take her down to 3,500 feet and see if we can't shed some of this ice. I know the de-icers are functional, but let's not take any chances," Trudeau said to his co-pilot.

"Agreed Skip, and once the de-icers help us out a bit, maybe we'll find some cleaner weather, and we can bring her back up a bit."

Neither aviator had to remind the other that the lower they flew the more fuel the thirsty bomber consumed. After adjusting altitude down to 3,500 feet, they broke through the clear air lying underneath the clouds. Miles and miles of nondescript gray sea stretched forever.

After a short period Trudeau said to Snavely, "Let's see if we can get above the cloud cover and try for a celestial fix," as he was growing more concerned by the minute. "Damn, if we could get up there, it'd help with fuel consumption." As he eased the yoke back, he could feel the mighty Pratt and Whitney's straining; the additional wing weight, due to ice, was keeping him from gaining substantial attitude. Trudeau thought, "Hell, if I could get up there, and get up into thinner air we'd be a lot better off. Too bad we couldn't get a fix for our oxygen gear."

By now Trudeau began to think of other options, as he had been trained to do. If they could climb enough to break through the ceiling, they were still confronted with the fact that they had problems with the crew oxygen tanks. This situation was getting nastier by the minute.

"Phil, we need to plot an alternative course of action. I need you to plot a course to Ireland, staying as far north as possible."

A few minutes later, Mills said, "Jim, I've a course plotted to the top of Northern Ireland, where I know there are a number of landing strips. The heading should be 120 degrees. I'm estimating we are about 1,200 miles WNW of Ireland at this point."

"Thanks Phil."

"Carl, I've made a decision. We are changing course to 120 degrees, and heading for Ireland right now."

"Skip, I agree. We know that if we go east we'll be in better shape, and there are just too many questions and radio problems out here." As Snavely finished talking, he could see on the ball that the

Damnyankee had already began a slow sweeping turn eastward.

Several hours passed as the *Damnyankee* remained resolutely directed toward Ireland. By this time, there was no question that tension had begun to build among the crew, as the seriousness of their situation became more apparent while the big plane droned tirelessly on over the Atlantic.

"Hey Jerry, what in hell is going on?" Frank Cicero had crawled over into a corner of the fuselage next to his pal Flecker, who was sitting calmly, rather morosely staring at the other side of the fuselage, no particular thoughts apparent in his mind.

"Y'know Frankie, I'm really not sure. I do know this much though. We've been with the Skip long enough to know that he knows what he's doing a hell of a lot better than any other guy on this bird, so my money stays on him. He's obviously decided that it makes more sense to head over towards Europe rather than fly around up in that damned Iceland/Greenland crap, depending on radio beams that don't ever seem to work. Hey man, at least we're heading in the direction of a lot more human beings, know what I mean?"

Cicero nodded his assent, reaching into his heavy flight jacket for a pack of Camels. He knocked the pack sharply on the deck, and a cigarette popped up as if out of a jack-in-the-box. He offered it to his buddy Flecker, and rapped it once more, bringing one up for himself. Flecker already had his Navy Zippo out, and both took a drag and expelled it into the cold atmosphere of the PB4Y-1 at almost exactly the same moment.

Fleucher continued to work like a madman over the radio controls, but was unable to obtain anything definitive. The *Damnyankee* continued to fly on, and by now fuel consumption was of paramount concern.

At around 1920 GMT, Trudeau tersely ordered Fleucher to begin transmitting a Mayday call over the emergency radio frequency.

Fleucher was finally able to pick up a weak but readable transmission from QDM Station NAGAR, in Nutt's Corner, Belfast. They advised the *Damnyankee* to alter course slightly by 10 degrees to portside.

Mills now estimated they had approximately two hours of fuel remaining, which might add up to around 350 miles. Apprehension and tension were building in the crew, but Trudeau was able to maintain discipline and focus.

These guys are a hell of a good crew, and all those hours of training are helping me to keep them functional, thought the now gravely-concerned pilot.

At 1930 GMT, Trudeau issued an order to the gunners to jettison all heavy non-essential gear in an effort to extend their range as far as possible. Beckwith, Lyle, Flecker, Cicero and Vigeant began to unceremoniously dump anything of substance that wasn't critical to the safety of the flight through the bomb bay as well as the waist gun ports.

On its way out, something slightly damaged the inner surface of the portside stabilizer after being jettisoned out the aft escape hatch, but it didn't seem to radically affect the plane's flight.

Then Trudeau issued orders to secure all loose equipment in the aircraft's interior. At around 2025 GMT, after more than a dozen hours in the air, Trudeau got on the intercom and addressed the crew.

"OK men, listen up. Our situation is serious, but definitely not hopeless. I want each of you to prepare for the possibility that we may have to ditch at sea within the next hour. We are all very well trained in those procedures, and I have absolute faith in the ability and qualifications of each and every one of you. There is not one question in my mind that I don't have the finest PB4Y-1 crew in the entire goddamned Navy, and we are going to get through this. You are a unit, and a very fine unit, and we are going to deal with whatever transpires in the same professional manner you have dealt with everything up to now. Go through your individual ditching situation duties in your mind, get your area policed and your gear prepared, and stand by to hear from me again. We are going to be just fine."

Jesus Christ, Trudeau thought, I sure hope I sounded like I believed what I was saying.

Trudeau was silently running and re-running the ditching procedure through his mind. He knew firsthand that the PB4Y-1 was an awkward duckling at best. He froze all other thoughts out of his mind, and tried to visualize the actual process. As he was slowly bringing the big white bird down closer to the sea, he knew that above all he had to keep the nose up, going into a stall just at the time of impact. Although it was by now far too dark to actually see, Trudeau was sure that he would encounter a stormy, roiling sea. That's OK, he thought; just keep the nose from ramming into the sea.

They passed through 1,000 feet, but still could see nothing in the ink-like void outside the cockpit. With the wind coming out of the northwest, he turned the aircraft so he would be heading straight into the wind when they made contact with the water.

At about 800 feet Trudeau rang the "execute ditching" bell. Fleucher, in businesslike fashion, calmly continued to transmit time and position repeatedly, so to have as accurate a possible final position to assist the Air-Sea-Rescue boys. Trudeau now dropped the wing flaps to further slow the aircraft.

"Snave, feather engines two and three," Trudeau barked. In perfect unison the co-pilot pulled back the throttle levers on the two inboard engines. As they passed through 600 feet, visibility cleared a bit, and they began to see, or at least sense, the surface of the ocean.

"Snave, fire two flares now."

Snavely did so, and both aviators slid back the side hatches they had so recently modified.

"OK, guys," Trudeau snapped over the intercom. "Brace yourselves, we are very close now."

Eddie Vigeant was scrunched down in his ditching position, and snatched a glance out the hatch.

"Jeezus H. Christ," he thought, "we're about five feet off the goddamned water!"

Vernon Peterson braced himself on the cabin deck, with Vigeant's legs on either side of him.

Trudeau struggled mightily with the bucking yoke as the aircraft began to lose stability, headway, and altitude. *Damnyankee* was now ten feet off the water with only 82 knots airspeed.

"Now!" he yelled to no one in particular, as he shoved both throttle levers forward, pulling back on the yoke simultaneously. The combination of both increased power and pitch brought the *Damnyankee's* nose up.

Trudeau felt the tail dip into the sea, easily slowing the craft. A split-second later the fuselage and nose plowed into the sea in a terrific bang. He would recall later that it felt exactly like "riding an eggshell into a concrete wall."

CHAPTER XI

IN THE WATER

Chaos. Wet chaos. Wet windy chaos. The windscreen of the PB4Y-1 had caved in on impact, and sea water was flooding into the cabin area. Trudeau felt great spasms of pain in his feet; the force of the impact into the sea had bent the rudder pedals back against them. Trudeau's seat had torn loose from the cockpit deck, and he was jammed up against the instrument panel and the pilot's yoke. He was already submerged and madly battling with the release buckle on his seat harness. While he was close to blacking out, he felt, or sensed Snavely thrashing around to his right, battling with his own release gear. Trudeau finally popped the seat harness, kicked off his flight boots, and pulled his feet from the twisted mass of metal that moments earlier had been the rudder pedals. Christ, he thought, at least we got the bird down.

"Snave, Snave, how are you doing?" Snavely gave him a shaky "thumbs up," and they both were able to slip out through Trudeau's recently reworked side panel, into the icy Atlantic. They emerged bobbing in the 20-foot waves almost simultaneously.

Everything ached on Trudeau, but oddly, the cold of the water took some of the immediate pain away from his badly bruised feet. He was unable to inflate his Mae West, as the pull cords had been tied together to prevent accidental inflation.

"Goddammit," he thought, "why in hell didn't I remember to untie them?"

During the struggle with his vest, he swallowed a lot of sea water, mixed with aviation fuel. Plus Trudeau, like all the crew, was in his flight suit, which soaked up water and acted like a sea anchor.

He knew they all had to get away from the plane and into the dinghies, and ASAP. He watched Snavely paddle towards the nose of the aircraft as he continued to fight the stubborn life vest. Snavely was bobbing up and down, not far from the hatch they had both scurried through. Trudeau wondered, amongst the wild wind and spray: how and where were the rest of the crew?

It looked to him like Mills and Peterson had somehow got out in front of the plane, but maybe only ten yards or so.

Back amidships, a dinghy appeared. The two dinghies, located in housings over the wings, should have automatically dropped out and inflated upon touching the sea.

Trudeau thrashed as well as he could toward the inboard portside engine cowling and hung on with both hands, trying to clear his head and assess the situation. His fingers were being slammed by the angry seas against the cowling and the engine it enclosed. He spotted Snavely in the water; the co-pilot appeared to be holding his own for the moment. At that moment Trudeau looked aft, and saw a dinghy bobbing crazily just behind the tail of the big plane.

"Come on Snave," Trudeau shouted. "There's a dinghy back here we can climb into."

With a mighty heave, Trudeau pulled himself atop the wing and looked back at Snavely. Now he didn't see him.

Vigeant had launched this dinghy through the portside waist hatch. With a mighty heave Trudeau pulled himself atop the wing, and looked back at Snavely. He didn't see him.

Oh Christ. What happened?

Maybe he went down the starboard side of the plane to hop in the other dink. Trudeau started vomiting from the mixture of aviation fuel and seawater he'd swallowed. About then he saw Cicero and Beckwith in the water along the side of the plane. Both were panicking because they were having trouble swimming.

Good God, Cicero had only barely learned to float.

Trudeau saw Peterson and Fleucher bobbing crazily in the heavy seas, their vests inflated. The skipper dragged himself slowly up on the wing, and then crawled down the spine of the bucking fuselage towards the dinghy, which was tethered to the tail of the plane. Between blasts of cold spray hurled at him, he could now see gunners Lyle, Vigeant and Cicero had made it into the dinghy.

As Trudeau struggled to keep his grip on the wild, pitching fuselage, inching ever closer to the tail, he saw Beckwith making his way into the bobbing craft. Trudeau reached the tail and immediately severed the dinghy's painter, in case the plane sank, dragging them down with it. Upon having the painter released from the tail, the winds immediately began to push the dinghy away from the plane.

Trudeau half jumped, half swam over to the dinghy, where Eddie Vigeant unceremoniously pulled him aboard. A short distance away, they found gunner Flecker floating on a bomb bay tank, and dragged him aboard the now heavily-ladened and wildly tossing dinghy.

"Quick fellas, let's see if the guys got into a dinghy on the other side," said Trudeau, between heaving over the side of the little craft.

They paddled, fiercely, for a half hour, but were only able to get within fifty yards of the plane. It was horrendous going, matching their exhausted bodies against the full force of the Atlantic winds. *Damnyankee* was still bobbing up and down in the seas. Trudeau could just make out its white hull in the half light. The crew, in shock to a man, and without strength following the ditching sat numbly in the dinghy.

After a few moments, Vigeant managed to extract an emergency whistle from his Mae West, and began to blow short, shrill blasts in the hope of stirring some response from the area of the plane. Cicero found his flashlight and tried to ply the water with its feeble beam, but to no avail. The dinghy, carrying only six of the crew, immediately began to drift with the wind, away from *Damnyankee.*

CHAPTER XII

ADRIFT IN THE NORTH ATLANTIC

A shroud of silence hung over the bucking craft, as the men began to think the unthinkable; their crewmates, their pals, could be gone for good. Trudeau, weak from nausea, began to face the fact that four of his ten crew members may be lost at sea: Carl Snavely, Phil Mills, Joe Fleucher, and Vernon Peterson.

Maybe, just maybe there was possibility that they were floating around in another dinghy, but those chances seemed slim. Vigeant himself had launched the dinghy the men were now in, through the portside waist hatch. Apparently the wing-stowed dinghies had malfunctioned and not released upon impact.

The six exhausted sailors bobbed up and down off the west coast of Ireland in their new home, an eleven foot by six and a half foot rubber inflatable life raft---the only thing between them and certain death in the North Atlantic.

The dinghy began to drift drunkenly away from the *Damnyankee,* which quickly faded into the murk. It was time to take stock of their situation.

They had lost the dinghy's entire emergency kit while wrestling it out the portside waist hatch. They also had no radio, nor did they have a Verie pistol to mark their existence for possible search planes. Affirming their location to any rescue efforts would be almost impossible. In essence, they had no food, no water, and no communication.

All of their flashlights had been soaked by now and were useless. Also, no one's watch still worked. The weather was poor, and showing little chance of improving, with no more than half a mile visibility. The seas were high and they weren't sure where they were ---hopefully off the coast of Ireland.

On the plus side, a quick inventory of the small craft showed a fishing kit, a patch kit, four paddles, a whistle, sail, sea anchor, mast, knives and some heavy weather clothing.

There was a feeling amongst the survivors that they might be drifting southward, paralleling the coastline. They were also aware of the tremendous danger of being swept away from land and out into the vast expanse of the Atlantic, where rescue would be highly unlikely.

That first night, as the seas built, they capsized for the first time.

They were already completely drenched with sea water, so the submersion did little to increase their discomfort. They found the cold penetrating if not numbing; it was difficult to retain body heat. Of course, the very fact that they were thrown from the dinghy into the wilds of the Atlantic greatly increased the danger of losing yet more crewmembers. Luckily, all six were recovered in short order, and made their way back into the little craft.

In the surprise, the crew lost two of the paddles, their pump, sail, sea anchor, mast and bailer.

An hour or so later, they were dumped into the sea a second time by a huge breaking wave. Again the survivors were all miraculously able to get back in the dinghy.

After the second capsize, they all agreed to hook their arms through the guide line along the inflatable's topsides, hoping this would keep them in contact with each other and the dink if they went over again.

Towards the end of the first night a number of crewmembers noted that Henry Beckwith was weakening. Trudeau and Lyle were both severely ill, vomiting repeatedly over the side. This of course, dehydrated them, and there was no way to replenish any of their body fluids.

Eventually the darkness of Thursday night began to be replaced by the dull gray of Friday morning, with the wind rising. They were still woefully misinformed as to their whereabouts, and had not much more than guesswork regarding their drift line.

Vigeant suddenly turned around and said, "Hey guys, look, there's an aircraft over the horizon!" The sea-battered inhabitants slowly, stiffly turned, following the direction of Eddie's finger and saw, sure enough, way over the horizon, the outline of an aircraft. It was too distant to ascertain what type of plane it might be. It continued away from them, finally disappearing over the horizon. A cloud of gloom descended over the tiny craft like a black funeral shroud.

"Goddammit," said Cicero, "Those hunkies didn't see us, and I don't even think they were looking for us."

Several murmurs or grumbles of agreement slipped out from the cold, wet crew, as they used their flight boots to scoop out water from the floor of the dinghy. The men were constantly surrounded by as much as a foot of cold sea water, sloshing around in the dinghy. That sizeable amount of water probably served to somewhat stabilize the small craft in heavy, breaking seas.

Eddie Vigeant seemed to have more strength than any of them. He and Beckwith had co-owned a dinghy, and he seemed the obvious one to handle the little boat.

Trudeau mumbled weakly to Vigeant. "Eddie, we need to try to set some sort of course. Maybe you can use my flight jacket as a sail."

Vigeant said, "Right, Skipper. We still have one paddle left, and we can use that as a rudder. Any kind of progress is better than nothing."

For the next seven hours, the crewmembers with any strength remaining held the jacket up to catch the wind, taking turns at clutching the unwieldy sail. At about noon, according to their guesstimates based on the sun's location, they noticed two huge seabirds, soaring over an object in the water. After awhile one of the birds landed on the water, not terribly far from the bobbing little craft.

"Wilbur, hand me that damned flashlight," said Vigeant.

Wilbur Lyle, looking curiously detached by now, reached over and fished the non-functional light up off the floor of the raft, where it had been rolling back and forth in the seawater, in what was about the only empty space on the floor of the raft.

"Here you go Eddie, but what in hell are you going to do with it?"

Vigeant grabbed the light from Lyle's hand, and said, "I used to be a pretty good baseball player, maybe I can hit this sucker with one of the batteries."

Flecker looked at Vigeant as if he were crazy, and said, "Eddie, what you gonna do, eat the damned thing?"

Vigeant said, "Hell no Jerry, I figure if we can kill this thing, with all of those feathers maybe we can somehow do something to fight this awful cold."

Needless to say, in a bobbing dinghy in a surging sea, Vigeant's efforts to brain the bird went to no avail.

At about 1400 hours on Friday, September 15th, the soggy crew's spirits rose quickly as they sighted land at a distance they calculated to be maybe ten to fifteen miles away. They would see it when the dinghy rode the crests of the waves, and it would disappear again as soon as they dropped into the troughs, only to appear once more as they rode the next crest.

With just a single paddle remaining, there was a sudden burst of energy, as they paddled with it, their hands and even shoes. This exhausted them further.

During the day they drifted closer, to within maybe three miles of the shore, only to pushed back to sea by the capricious tides off the West of Ireland.

Now self-doubt began to creep into their weary minds, and some of them began to question whether they had actually sighted land, or if it was nothing more than an illusion.

After they had recovered a bit from the excitement and exhaustion of the effort to reach shore, Flecker leaned over to Trudeau and muttered, "Skipper, if we're drifting down the coast of Ireland, there's nothing to prevent us from floating right past the island, and then out to sea again. Is there anything we can do to try to direct the drift to our advantage?"

Trudeau thought for a minute and repositioned himself in the stern of the bobbing little craft, using the sole paddle as a makeshift tiller. In time, it seemed like the jury-rigged tiller was beginning to help move them in the direction they surmised land to be.

"Jerry, I think your idea might be working," said Trudeau. "Maybe we can switch helmsmen from time to time, with anyone who still feels they have any strength remaining."

Shortly after, however, Vigeant blurted out, "Hey fellas, this damned dink is leaking. Look at how the starboard side is beginning to buckle!"

Sure enough, there was a definite weakening of the starboard air compartment, which was allowing in even more seawater.

"Jeezus H. Christ, we gotta fix it right now, or we're all goners!" said Frank Cicero.

Wilbur Lyle said, "Here, I'm going to go over the side and find the leak. Be sure you keep your eye on me, and break out that patch kit while I look for the leak."

Good old Lyle, taking charge of the maintenance of their tiny rubber home just as he had over the *Damnyankee*. Into the water he went, submerging under the dinghy briefly, looking for the leak, and then surfacing, gasping for air. Vigeant kept a grip on any part of Wilbur he could hang on to. After about three or four submersions, the determined crewman came back to the surface and said, "I found the dirty little bugger. Give me a patch, and I'll go under and fix her. Eddie, keep hold of me!"

They handed Lyle a patch and once more he went under the dinghy, this time for what seemed like forever. He finally burst back to the surface, panting mightily in an attempt to fill his lungs with fresh air.

"I got it. I think I got it. We should be OK now!"

With some difficulty Vigeant and Cicero helped horse Lyle up over the gunwale. For several minutes he just lay across the legs of his crew mates, trying to regain strength. Vigeant looked around and said, to nobody in particular, "Where is that damned fishing kit? That bastard is what probably put the hole in the dink. Find it for me!"

After some weak fumbling around in the watery floor, Frank Cicero came up with the fishing rig. "Here it is Eddie, what do you want to do with it?"

Vigeant said, "Give it to me, Frank." As soon as he did, Vigeant unceremoniously pitched it, hook, line and all, over the side of the dinghy.

"Sonofabitch was gonna sink us," muttered Vigeant to nobody, as he wrenched his body around in an effort to try to retain some warmth.

A deep silence settled in over the crew. Delirium began to creep upon them. The cold was intense, penetrating every fiber of each man in the bobbing little craft.

Trudeau, weakened as he was by stomach problems, knew that he had to keep them awake, lest anyone lapse into a coma. That could spell lethal trouble.

Trudeau thought oddly that he wasn't all that hungry, and that he would trade the largest Thanksgiving meal he'd ever had for the chance to be warm and dry for even a few minutes.

Lyle had recovered somewhat from his patching adventure, but he and Trudeau were repeatedly retching over the side of the dinghy. This incessant vomiting continued to degrade both of them.

Before long Vigeant noticed that Trudeau himself was weakening, and lapsed into delirium on occasion, muttering about the crew, and protecting them. Everybody was feeling the terrible affects of the numbing cold and wetness. The cloud ceiling had dropped to about 300 feet, and a slight but steady rain fell.

At about 1600 hours on Friday they once more sensed the presence of land, then saw it too. The benumbed crew members who were still semi-functional estimated they were again maybe 20 miles offshore.

Cicero suddenly began fumbling around under his legs, and came up with a sodden oil cloth map. "Look at this damned thing, where did it come from? It's some kind of map."

Vigeant looked at it and said, "I'll be damned. It's a survival map of Europe. They use them for downed crews. I wonder where this thing was hiding?"

Trudeau muttered to Vigeant that maybe they should use it as a makeshift sail, and that two guys could hold it to catch the wind, in an effort to move them more rapidly towards the shore. Vigeant and Cicero held the oilcloth map on either side of the small raft, and although it was taxing their already weakened bodies, it did in fact seem to help propel the dinghy. Vigeant and Cicero took turns trading off with Flecker and Lyle in keeping the crude sail aloft as well as they could. As darkness began to descend upon their second day at sea, they once more spotted land.

"Skipper, look, land! I think we're closer." Frank Cicero pointed off to the east. One more time, the exhausted crew rose to the occasion and began paddling frantically with hands and shoes to try to approach the shore. They could actually see a small cottage near the shore, glowing almost translucently in that haunting afterlight of the west coast of Ireland.

But wind and treacherous tides began once more to sweep them out to sea. It was almost too much to bear. The emotional effect of getting so close, and then having conditions turn on them yet again, weighed as heavily as a load of concrete on the dispirited, group of men.

They were all weak from hunger and exhaustion. In reality, the crew had not eaten properly since their departure from Norfolk, which now seemed eons ago, but was actually only a little more than a week before.

At one point during the night, after being unconscious for some time, Trudeau awoke to an apparition of a hatless but immaculately uniformed American G.I. sitting in the bow of the dinghy. The G.I. appeared to alternate his position from the bow to the stern of the little craft. It seemed like he was beckoning to Trudeau to come forward, to follow him. He radiated most clearly in Trudeau's vision, and alternately pointed to various pinpricks of light as they may have been drifting into a bay, and identified them alternately as "Norway, Ireland, and Iceland."

Frank Cicero saw much the same hallucination, an extra man in the dinghy. He pointed toward the bow and asked, "Where in hell did you come from?"

Of course, there was no answer.

"Skipper, Henry is looking pretty awful."

Sure enough, Beckwith's skin had a bluish pallor, his face slowly beginning to turn ashen white. He was breathing with increasing difficulty. Clearly the relentless cold and dehydration was taking its toll on him more than anyone else.

"Do what you can to keep him comfortable," said Trudeau, himself in poor shape.

"I've got an idea," said Flecker. "I'm drenched anyway, and don't know how I could get any colder. I'll slip over the side and tie myself in on the gunwale ropes. This'll make more room inside the raft. Maybe we can lift Henry up off the floor, and stretch him out over your guys' legs," he said, pointing to both Lyle and Vigeant.

"Let's keep Henry out of the water as much as we can. That way we might be able to keep him a little warmer."

Without hesitation, Flecker lowered himself over the side, wrapping his left arm around the rope along the top of the portside inflated gunwale. After an initial gasp, he said he didn't seem to feel much different than he did inside the dinghy. At least he was out of the cutting wind.

Lyle and Vigeant maneuvered stiffly around to pull the nearly comatose Beckwith up onto their legs.

"C'mon Henry, we'll get you out of that water. Eddie and I are going to take care of you," Lyle whispered. Beckwith's eyes fluttered in acknowledgement.

Around midnight on Friday they again spotted what they thought had to be a lighthouse in the distance. Each felt some comfort and redemption as they saw the beam from the light sweeping methodically over the black expanse that engulfed them. Somewhere around 0430 on Saturday morning, September 16th, Henry Beckwith lost his battle for life. He died quietly, and with dignity, slipping off one of his crewmates legs into the sloshing water.

It was a few minutes before the groggy Lyle noticed a difference.

"Eddie, Eddie, I think we may have lost Henry."

"Skipper, Skipper, I think Henry may be gone," Eddie Vigeant said.

Trudeau crawled over to the motionless body of Beckwith, and began to attempt to resuscitate him.

"Henry, Henry, come on, we're here with you. Stay with us, Henry."

It didn't work.

Trudeau visibly sagged as he laid Beckwith gently back on the bottom of the dinghy, and allowed himself to flop back against the inflated gunwale. There was an incomprehensible look of grief in Trudeau's eyes.

"He's gone, fellas, Henry is gone."

Whatever strength had remained in Trudeau's voice was gone, too, and the words came out as a dull, unearthly pronouncement.

It was just too much. Trudeau realized those who had been watching over Beckwith, as he struggled for life, had themselves lapsed into unconsciousness from time to time. It may well have been that the young airman drowned in the water constantly roiling around the floor of the sagging dinghy.

Briefly they spoke about what should be done with his body. Trudeau was adamant that they keep it with them.

With great difficulty the crew placed Beckwith in the bottom of the dinghy, with as much dignity as possible, his arms folded over his chest.

"C'mon Jerry, it's back in the boat with you," muttered Vigeant hoarsely.

Flecker was almost incapable of movement. His skin was also taking on a bluish pallor.

"Get Jerry tucked in between you. You have to keep his temperature up." Trudeau, exhausted after even that perfunctory sentence, sagged back once more against the side of the wet inflatable.

His crewmates struggled to get Flecker into a position propped against them, so he might absorb whatever heat he could from their own cold upper bodies.

Eventually Flecker began to shiver a bit, which Vigeant took as a good sign.

"Hey Jerry, don't worry about the shivering. It means your body is trying to re-heat itself."

Flecker looked at Vigeant and nodded.

Trudeau began to hallucinate. Once he muttered about the coast of Iceland.

By now, most of the crew members were slipping in and out of hallucinatory spells.

The little craft appeared to circle the lighthouse on the shore more than once, helpless in the grasp of the swirling, vicious tides. The crew couldn't paddle anymore. Sometime after they realized Henry Beckwith had died, the dinghy ran up on a low rocky shelf. It was the first time they had touched land in two days.

Several of the men clambered out and fell drunkenly out over the sagging inflatable gunwales. They weren't on a beach, though, and it was soon clear that the seaweed-covered slimy rock was fast disappearing under a flood tide.

With monumental effort, the rest of the crew hauled themselves out. They somehow marshalling the strength to dump the seawater from the dinghy, and then laid Beckwith's body back in as gently as possible. They shoved off from the spit of rock. Almost immediately, knowing they had to take advantage of the rapid flood tide in an effort to reach the mainland.

It had to be close.

"Look. Look, there's a blinking light. It's got to be the shore."

As they strained to see, sure enough, the light blinked again, about 90 degrees off the portside. It charged them enough to once more paddle.

"Where in hell do you think that light is coming from?" Cicero asked.

"I dunno, maybe it's some kind of night patrol," Vigeant said, never taking his eyes off the last spot he'd seen the light.

Vigeant began to use the whistle still hanging around his neck to blast an SOS signal in Morse code. Before long the blinker was telegraphing back a letter "R", which meant message received. Vigeant continued to issue his SOS distress call on the whistle, and they kept getting the "received" message back from the light. Suddenly the light stopped moving, and was turned directly toward them.

Could someone on the beach have heard them? Maybe the wind blew the sound?

They kept paddling. Exhausted though they were, they dug a little deeper into themselves and each of the five survivors somehow mined one last vein of strength. Now they used their hands as cups to propel the craft toward shore.

At about 0630 on Saturday, September 16th, the little dinghy washed up on the Irish coast with a resounding crunch. It slid over some gravel and lurched to a sodden stop.

CHAPTER XIII

LANDFALL IN THE WEST OF IRELAND

After 33 hours of being slammed about incessantly by the fury of the autumn Atlantic, their first inclination was to rest, to just rest and doze. Trudeau, ever the officer and leader, even in his weakened state, realized they needed help, and they needed it now. Vigeant appeared to be in the best shape of any of them, and he volunteered to accompany Trudeau in his search for assistance. Having lost his shoes to the bent rudder pedals at the time of the ditching, Trudeau had no choice but to take the shoes from Beckwith's body, as he would be otherwise unable to negotiate the rocky beach.

After making sure the dinghy was securely pulled up and beached, Trudeau and Vigeant began half-walking, half-crawling along the shore in their search for help. The rest of the crew needed little encouragement to stay with the craft, as they were completely spent.

The beleaguered seamen were never able to trace the source of the light they had seen from the dinghy, but there was no question amongst them that they had seen it.

It was still dark along the rocky little inlet, and Trudeau and Vigeant were stumbling and crawling across the rocks when Trudeau suddenly slipped away and fell several feet off one rock, cracking his head on another just below him.

Vigeant heard a sickening thud, and turned around and half slid, half fell over the rock where he found Trudeau laying motionless on a wet patch of sand.

"Skipper, are you okay?"

After a moment or two Trudeau rolled over and tried to focus on the barely visible face of Vigeant. Slowly the young gunner came into a fuzzy focus in the dark grayness of the pre-dawn's thinnest light.

"Oh man, it feels like someone really beaned me. What happened, Eddie?"

"I think you must have slipped, and I sure heard you crack your head. Sounded like a rifle shot."

"Eddie, we've got to find some help, and right now." Slowly, and with great difficulty Trudeau began to crawl back onto the coastal rocks. "We need to find a house, so we can get someone to help our guys."

The two men continued to crawl up off the beach, off the rocks, and onto a sandy spit covered with sawgrass.

"Skipper, look, does that shadow look like a house?" Trudeau's eyes strained through the last of the darkness, and he wasn't sure what Eddie was seeing. He thought his eyesight might be impaired from the nasty fall he'd taken, and then, ever so imperceptibly, he sensed as much as saw the shape of a small house off in the darkness.

"Eddie, I think I see it. I think I see the house you're talking about. Oh God, do you think we can get over there?"

"Sure Skipper, I know we can get there. Let's get going, and be sure we don't fall into any more holes in the ground."

The two continued their farcical half-crawl, half-walk in the direction of what they felt was a house, or at least a building. Slowly, as they inched closer, and as the dawn began to signal its arrival, the outline of a cottage began to appear, just slightly lighter at first, and then darker than the background of the just-awakening day.

As they crawled up to the front door, Vigeant helped Trudeau to his feet, and they knocked on the door.

"Hello, hello in there. Can you help us? We are Americans. Can you help us? Hello. Hello."

Trudeau was just about spent. The effort to arouse someone inside the cottage was further exhausting him. They sensed there was someone inside, someone on the other side of the door, but nobody came. Trudeau leaned slightly on Vigeant, and there was no question that he was still wobbly.

"God Eddie, we've got to get help. I've got to get someone to help our guys on the beach."

Vigeant squinted for a second, and said, "Skipper. Skipper, look. There's another cottage, a small one. Right over there. Let's go."

Trudeau and his young bow gunner began to walk across the

rugged ground, looking not unlike two late night revelers, weaving, stumbling their way home. When they reached this cottage, with the light improving now, they could see how tiny it was, with a thatched roof atop the little stone building.

Vigeant rapped on the sturdy little door. "Hello. Hello. Is there anyone in there? We need help. We're American aviators. We need help!"

Suddenly, in the emerging dawn, the cottage door flew open and a man came out, brandishing what looked like a pitchfork. He jabbed it in the direction of Vigeant, backing him up against the wall with the fork at his neck.

"Hold it, hold it, man," Vigeant yelled, extending his hands out, palms up. "Easy, easy. We aren't looking for trouble. We're Americans."

"Sir, we're Americans, we are with the United States Navy. We mean you no harm. We need your help." Jim Trudeau, in spite of the agony he was in, sounded like he was in command of the situation.

"I know, ye're from out of the sea," was the answer, in a thick West of Ireland brogue.

CHAPTER XIV

ASHORE AT AILLEABREACH

He slowly leveled the pitchfork to the ground, and then placed it against the stone wall of the cottage. It was evident the man, a bachelor of 55 years named Michael Conneely, realized that these men were not a danger, but in fact were in great danger of keeling over themselves, by the look of them.

"Come in then, come in and warm yerselves."

Conneely immediately set to stoking the turf fire in the tiny cottage. Before long, Trudeau and Vigeant felt some relief from being away from the wretchedness of the icy Atlantic. Conneely gave them large, coarse blankets. They removed their soaking wet clothes, and wrapped themselves in the rough covers. Ever so slowly they began to feel the blood creeping back into their extremities. The man offered the Yanks some Irish brown bread. Trudeau, still sick from the aviation fuel, picked at it, but Vigeant ate the hearty slices ravenously. The man offered them some whiskey to wash it down with. It seared like molten fire on Trudeau's gasoline-damaged throat. The pilot struggled to get up, but collapsed back against the wall, wrapped in his blanket, close to the fire.

"Men…we've got men with us, and they need help. They need help right now. Our raft is ashore…..not far from here. My men are weak… exhausted…we need help for them. There are three men still in the raft, and we have one man that died. Henry. Henry Beckwith…Henry didn't make it."

Conneely straightaway rushed out the door, leaving Trudeau and Vigeant recovering by the fire. He headed, they soon found out, to Martin O'Malley's house for help. Martin lived not 150 yards up the road, and was a friend of Michael Conneely's.

Martin was a Seagull, (which the Irish pronounced with the first syllable rhyming with day), part of the Irish coastal defense team: Michael thought he would know what to do to help the Americans. Besides, the Dunhill lookout post, which Martin had access to, had one of only two telephones in the area, the other being at the Ballyconneely Post Office, which would surely not be open at this hour.

On the way, Michael was in such a rush that he lost a boot. Running along with one bare foot didn't slow his progress, however.

Martin O'Malley was assigned to the Dunhill lookout post, LOP # 53, situated atop a hill overlooking the Atlantic, behind the castle ruins of Grainne O'Maille, the Irish pirate queen who lived during the fifteenth century. Martin was home now, still asleep, having come off duty about 2000 hours the night before. He dressed quickly, pulled on his boots, and ran back up the hill in the light of early dawn to Dunhill to raise the alarm.

It was a steep climb up to the lookout post; Martin had done it so often it seemed hardly a bother. Paddy King and Johnny O'Neill were the two Saygulls on watch. Martin told them what he knew about what had happened, and immediately grabbed the phone.

The outside world first found out about the fate of the *Damnyankee* crew by that telephone call made from the lonely little concrete observation box atop a wind-battered hill overlooking Ballyconneely Bay. The call was made to Joe Davitt, the night telephone operator in Clifden, and he put the call through to Clifden 8, the Garda Station, which was about eight miles from the Dunhill post.

After asking Paddy King at the Garda station to call Galway 56 (the Army Barracks), Martin bounded back down the hill to Conneely's cottage.

Martin realized that he must launch an immediate search for the survivors. Borrowing the survival whistle off Trudeau's vest, he set off for the shoreline to see what he could find. He hadn't gone more than several hundred yards when he saw the water-logged, half-deflated life raft dragged up on the shore. In it were three survivors, barely conscious, and Henry Beckwith's body, which had not yet stiffened.

Martin rolled the three aviators out onto the beach as gently as he could, and then dragged the dinghy up out of the tide zone, with Beckwith still in it. Then, with the help of his brother Jimmy, Martin half-dragged, half-carried, and generally herded the three exhausted sailors up the beach to Conneely's cottage.

By this time the turf fire was crackling and glowing, the cottage was warming, and they hurriedly stripped the soaked uniforms off the three men. They too were wrapped in coarse, heavy wool blankets, and hot tea was served. It was the first nourishment the men had taken in almost forty hours.

After a few minutes, Jerry Flecker turned to Frank Cicero and said weakly, "You know something Frankie? I don't think there'll ever be a beer or a cocktail for the rest of my life that could taste half as good as this mug of tea." Cicero turned his head slowly toward Flecker and said, "Jerry I think you just might be right about that. This is one time I won't argue with you."

As previously scheduled, Martin O'Malley and J. King took over the watch at the Dunhill LOP at precisely 0800 on Saturday, September 16th, 1944. They dutifully entered the names of the survivors in the LOP log as entry number 845.

At precisely the same time that O'Malley was recording the names into the log, the first Garda contingent from Clifden was arriving at Conneely's.

Martin Egan, Peadar Walsh and Pat Fox arrived first, along with the Chief Superintendent and another Garda, Mulgrew. Then a Red Cross ambulance pulled up, with a young Red Cross Sergeant Olive Harley, and medical helpers Tom McDonald, Jo Moran and Michael McInerny. Clifden physician Willie Casey Jr. arrived from his home immediately following the ambulance. The young Doctor Casey had been deputized for the occasion by his father, the senior physician in Clifden.

By now the little bayside community of Ailleabreach was becoming a busy place, particularly for so early in the morning. The storm of the previous day had abided, and it promised to be a clear day.

A number of children had begun to accumulate along the beach, exhibiting a genuine feeling of excitement over anything as unusual as this happening in their village. The rumor that a dead body was on the beach only stimulated their curiosity further.

"C'mon," said young Josie O'Malley, a seven year-old villager, to several friends. "Let's get down to the beach…I heard me Da say there was a real dead person down there…just layin' in the raft like he was takin' a wee snooze."

With considerable anticipation the group of four lads went down to the beach, only to be rebuffed by John O'Neill, a volunteer who had been stationed there to guard the body of Henry Beckwith.

"G'wan, get ye out of here, ye pack of scavengers, before I have to take after ye. This is no place at a time like this for a group of young slackers like ye to be nosin' around this poor dead soul. Jaysus, Mary and Joseph…give the poor man some respect, and let him lay here in peace." Dismayed, the boys turned away.

"Didja see him…didja see him…the dead one?" asked Josie.

"I believe I did…I think he was that dark thing alayin' there on the sand. Dead he looked, and that's the truth!"

CHAPTER XV

RECOVERY IN THE CLIFDEN COTTAGE HOSPITAL

The five Americans were driven by John Payne to the Clifden Cottage Hospital, a distance of about eight miles. Payne served double duty as a hackney driver and as an undertaker, from his home on Main Street in Clifden. Olive Harley and the other Red Cross volunteers followed him to the Clifden hospital, where they administered to the survivors.

After seeing to it that the five survivors were safely ensconced in the hands of the good Sisters of Mercy at the Clifden hospital, Payne stopped long enough at his place of business to gather a coffin, then turned back down the coast road to Ailleabreach. where he proceeded to coffin the body of Beckwith right. He placed Beckwith's body in the coffin right on the beach.

As the young aviator had been identified by the crew as belonging to the Protestant faith, Payne delivered his remains to the Church of Ireland in Clifden, where the body was received and greeted with a few simple prayers. Later that day a certificate of death was provided by Mrs. King, assistant registrar for the Church of Ireland in Clifden.

Much of the excitement in Ailleabreach was now gone, with the removal of both the survivors and Beckwith's corpse. John O'Neill and Martin O'Malley deflated the battered dinghy, folding it as best they could and placing it in the boot of Paddy Carbery's car. Paddy drove off shortly, under the directions of the Irish Army.

While the village was swiftly returning to the quiet place it had been prior to that morning, the crew of the *Damnyankee* were beginning yet another phase of their adventure.

First, the five Navy men were assisted up the hospital's seventeen front steps to the main entrance. Still much weakened from their ordeal, the survivors were more than happy to be admitted to a warm, centrally-heated ward already occupied by three other patients.

Within a few minutes of getting settled in to beds, they were visited by several nuns and a nurse.

"Gentlemen" began one nun, the leader of the group. "We feel blessed to be able to offer a helping hand to ye. Understanding what ye've been through, we hope to make you as comfortable during yer stay here as we can. This is Sister Carmel, and this is Sister Aloysius. I'm Sister Mercy. Nurse Glynn will also be looking after ye.

"Glory be to God that ye've made it here, safe out of the sea. We'll try our best to make yer stay here as comfortable as we are able to."

The aviators mumbled their thanks and appreciativeness. After delivering a few instructions on how things worked at the hospital, the nuns and nurse Glynn backed out of the ward to offer the men some privacy.

In short time, two of the sisters entered the ward with hot tea and brown bread with butter. Some of the men ate a bit, but Trudeau and Lyle were in no shape or mood to eat. All of them were weak, Trudeau in particular.

They spoke softly together, without humor. Despite the relief at having been saved from the sea, these men had gone through too much, and were too numb over the loss of their crewmates for much conversation. The exhausted men bore little resemblance to the jocular, cocky crew of just a few days earlier. Drained physically and emotionally, they realized their mates were gone forever. The experience had aged them beyond their years; the weight of it settling upon them like a cold, sticky fog.

Trudeau thrashed around restlessly in his bed before finally succumbing to the weariness that was stalking each of them. From time to time his fitful sleep would be interrupted by a racking cough as his body struggled to rid itself of the foreign substances he had swallowed.

Sister Mercy entered the ward in mid-afternoon, following a polite rap on the doorjamb.

"Ye've got a pair of visitors to see ye. I believe ye know Doctor Willie Casey. 'Twas he who looked after you down at the beach, and after ye came to us. He is also with Commandant John Power, from the Irish Army. I'll send them in a few minutes."

After she left, the men made a half-hearted effort to make themselves look a bit more presentable.

After a moment Doctor Casey entered, along with a tall, gaunt gentleman with dark hair, dressed in an English-looking military uniform.

"Well, it's a bit better you're looking than a few hours ago," the physician said with a smile. "Gentlemen, this is Commandant John Power. He is stationed at Athlone, and is in charge of the Army here in the West of Ireland. He wanted to see you, and I told him a bit about your adventure, and that you'd need several days to recuperate here in our hospital."

Power flashed a quick look at Casey, and asked who was in charge. Trudeau identified himself as the pilot and skipper of the aircraft. He began to answer Power's questions as well as he could about the ditching and subsequent happenings off the coast. He was forced to stop repeatedly to catch his breath.

Power was certainly polite, but Trudeau sensed that the Irish officer might be a bit uneasy at having five Yanks unceremoniously dropped upon him. After Trudeau had filled Power in on as much detail as he could remember, the Irish Commander smiled after shaking each of their hands, and told them he hoped they'd get some rest as soon as possible. After shaking Trudeau's hand one final time, Power turned on his heel and disappeared out the door of the ward.

In the early evening, as he headed towards a bathroom, Jerry Flecker noticed a tall, angular, well-muscled man sitting on a chair outside their ward. On the way back he introduced himself to the gentleman. After Flecker told Trudeau about his meeting in the hallway, Trudeau struggled to get up, wrapped himself in the robe the sisters had provided, and shuffled out the doorway.

"Hello, my name's Captain Trudeau, I'm the pilot and the man in charge of our crew here." Trudeau held out his hand, and the Irishman sprung up out of the chair and grasped it with a vise-like grip. Trudeau thought he might be a fisherman; for sure this hand belonged to a man who had seen plenty of hard work.

"Hello, hello, it's fine to meet you, it is."

"Why are you outside our door?" asked Trudeau, with as

pleasant a look as he could force upon his face.

"Well now, it's not every day we get a pack of Yanks dropped in on us now, is it?" said the Garda man, with a toothy smile. "Someone has to look after ye, and see that ye aren't bothered, so ye can gain your strength back."

"Are you from around here," asked Trudeau.

"Aye, I'm an islander," answered the man.

"An islander," responded Trudeau.

"Aye, yes. I come from the Aran Islands, off the coast of Galway. Irishman, to be sure."

Trudeau nodded, thanked the man, turned and began to work his way back toward his bed.

I wonder why he's here, thought the pilot. Do you suppose they feel a need to guard us? The islander was pleasant enough, and in no way threatening, but Trudeau felt there was more to his presence than a simple chair ornament.

Ireland was neutral in this war, as in the last, thought Trudeau, as he climbed back into bed. He wondered what might be in store for him and the remaining members of his crew. He had sensed slightly nervous vibrations from his visit with Commandant Power of the Irish Army. What did it all mean? Before long, the weariness of the past few days crept over him, and he fell asleep.

A bit later a slight commotion woke Trudeau. He slowly rolled over to see a young woman having entered the room, and in conversation with several of his men. She looked familiar to him. Talking softly with the men, she reached into a parcel she carried, finding several packets of cigarettes, which the crewmembers readily accepted.

"Hallo, captain, and how are ye feeling after a bit of rest?" asked the pleasant young woman.

"I'm fine, thank you and…"

Before Trudeau could finish, the girl broke in…

"Captain, my name is Olive Harley, and I'm a Red Cross volunteer. I was there at the beach this morning to assist ye and yer men. With all ye've been through, I wouldn't expect ye to recognize me…"

"Why Olive, I do remember you. You have a kind face. And what did you bring us?"

"Ah captain, it isn't much, it isn't, but I was able to round up a few packs of smokes at the Red Cross Center, and I thought it might be good to bring them over to ye lads."

The crew was happy to see Olive and her lovely smile. Before long they were all chatting in one corner of the ward. She was an attractive young woman, a fact that wasn't lost for a moment on the young sailors. Young men and a young woman, thought Trudeau. Well good for her, and thank God for people like Olive Harley. It would do the men some good to have a chance to talk with her a bit.

The food at the hospital was simple but good fare, and their strength began to return throughout the day. Following breakfast the next morning, four of the men dressed themselves in clothing donated by the villagers, and left the hospital for the first time.

Accompanied by Commandant Power and several others, they walked across the little town of Clifden to the Church of Ireland. It was an imposing building in such a small town, standing like a sentinel, as did the Catholic Church on the other side of town. The first edifice on the Church of England site had been built in 1812, a third of a century before the Great Famine, which had so horribly decimated Ireland, and particularly the west. This region, and for that matter all of Connacht, had been the scene of countless tragedies. This church had replaced much of the original building in 1853; it was designed to seat about 120 people.

Henry Beckwith's body had remained overnight in the church, and now lay at the foot of the chancel steps in the coffin John Payne had provided the day before. It was a proper coffin, made of oak, and fully lined.

As Reverend Edward Griffin, the normal Rector, had departed earlier in the year, Commandant Power had arranged for a visiting clergyman, named Reverend O'Connell, to hold a short memorial service for the young airman.

O'Connell was on holiday from the Rectory in Tullamore. Because of his informal purpose for being in Clifden, arrangements had been made to borrow clerical vestments from the local Catholic priest, Canon Cunningham. There was a small group of locals in attendance, including the good Sisters of Mercy, Doctor Casey, Olive Harley and nurse Glynn.

Trudeau was still too weak to attend. The other surviving *Damnyankee* crewmembers gathered together in the old church, heads down and caps in hand as the Reverend said a few brief prayers. Following the service, the men filed by Beckwith's coffin, one by one, each taking a moment to remember their crewmate in his own way, pausing for a prayer or lightly touching the coffin.

Outside the church, an Irish Army ambulance swung around and pulled up near the entrance. Several soldiers and townspeople helped lift the coffin of the airman into the back of the lorry. Captain Burthistle, another Irish Army officer, seemed to be everywhere at once, and it was he who handled many of the arrangements for Beckwith's body. Burthistle moved around to the left front door, and entered it alongside the driver. The driver ground the lorry into gear, and with a puff of blue smoke, the lorry began the first leg of Henry Beckwith's final journey, this time to the border at the north of Ireland for transfer to the proper authorities.

The crew was quiet as they returned to the hospital. About late morning, brothers Jimmy and Martin O'Malley paid a visit to the Americans, some of whom were feeling well enough to be walking all around the little hospital.

"Well lads, it's a bit better yer looking' than ye were when we fished ye off the beach down at Ailleabreach," said Jimmy, the younger of the O'Malley brothers.

There was a great shaking of hands all around. Martin had been the fellow that initiated the rescue. Young Jimmy had brought some whiskey to warm them up at Michael Conneely's cottage.

Eddie Vigeant recognized Jimmy O'Malley instantly.

"You came all the way into town to check up on us. How did you get here?"

"Well now, we both rode in on a pair of horses."

"Horses? Really, you came in on horses?"

"Why yes, we did. You see, I haven't the price of a bicycle, so we rode in on the horses to see ye."

It wasn't a joke, however. Things west of the Shannon had always been bleak from a financial standpoint, and Jimmy wasn't kidding when he said he couldn't afford a bicycle. Enthused to see the O'Malley's, the Americans peppered them with questions on details they might recall of the crew's arrival on the shore. Although it'd happened less than two full days earlier, it seemed eons ago.

After a spirited visit, the O'Malley brothers said they must be on their way back down the coast; the Irishmen left, knowing fully how much the *Damnyankee* crew appreciated all they had done for them.

CHAPTER XVI

DINNER AT DOCTOR CASEY'S

On Sunday night, Doctor Willie Casey had invited the survivors to dine with him.

The crew was excited at the prospect of getting out of the hospital for a reason more cheerful than Henry's prayer service. An hour before they were to be picked up by the doctor, Commandant Power made another appearance. The men gathered together to hear what the Irish Army officer had to say.

"Gentlemen, I have some news for you. As you know, Ireland has chosen to remain neutral in this war. While we have long enjoyed a fine relationship with your country, having you here past your convalescence is simply not practical, nor is it right. I wanted to tell you this in person. A decision has been made at the highest level to turn you over to the American authorities as soon as it is possible." The sailors all looked at each other, wondering what would happen next.

"Excuse me, Commandant, but I would like a few details as to this decision. When will it happen? Where will it happen and how?" Everyone in the ward turned and looked at Trudeau.

"Lieutenant, I am afraid I am not free to explain any details, but suffice it to say that we want to get this accomplished as soon as possible. This is a difficult situation for the government of Ireland, as I am sure you must realize. In the meantime, we shall do our best to treat you as well as possible, and I shan't think it'll be too long now. That is all I can say at this time."

Power spun on his heels and walked smartly out of the room, leaving nothing more than the sound of his shoes clicking on the well-scrubbed wooden floor as he passed down the hall and out the entrance of the hospital.

"Jerry, where do you think they're sending us?" asked Vigeant of Flecker.

"For God's sake Eddie, whadda I look like, a fortune teller? How should I know? It's a cinch they weren't going to leave us here forever. Anyway, sounds like we'll know something more in the next day or so."

Trudeau fretted. Although he was beginning to regain his strength, his pacing of the room was reduced to a slow walking around its perimeter. He well knew that wherever they went and whatever happened, these were his men, and they were his responsibility. He felt good about that. He stopped and looked at the four crewmembers. This was one hell of a good group of men, he thought, and he'd do his level best to continue to lead them as well he could.

"Come on fellas; let's get ready to go over to the Doc's for dinner. You know we're probably in for a great evening. Let's look as sharp as we can."

Trudeau wanted to get their attention off the uncertainties that lay ahead, and the dinner at the doctor's home could help him accomplish just that. With their donated clothing, they might not look particularly military, but at least they were wearing clean clothes.

The *Damnyankee* crew members were in high spirits as they waited to be picked up outside the little hospital. In a matter of a few minutes, the doctor came around the corner and up the hill in a small black English Ford. It was a tight squeeze. On the way, Flecker told Cicero he was reminded of a circus he'd attended in Brooklyn as a youngster, where it seemed an entire platoon of clowns had stuffed themselves into one little vehicle.

Doctor Casey told the men his home was called "Villa Maria." The crew wondered what that might imply. As they unfolded from the car, Vigeant tugged on Flecker's sleeve long enough to pull him back from the crowd heading up the front steps. "Jeezus Jerry, it looks like our digs are improving tonight. What in hell do you suppose they'll feed us?"

"I don't know, country, but do me a favor and don't embarrass me. You upstate hicks better remember to eat with a knife and fork, and not just your hands." Vigeant took a fake swing at Flecker, who ducked, laughing as he did so.

It was a fine meal. The Casey's served lamb roast, with potatoes and parsnips. The survivors of the *Damnyankee* ate like there'd be no tomorrow. The setting was inspiring to the men as well.

"Eddie, have you ever seen anything as beautiful as the walls in this dining room?"

Flecker raised his napkin so everyone didn't hear his comment.

"I don't think I've ever seen a room with such fine purple walls as this. They're the color of wine. And look at the beautiful woodwork on the wall over there. Good God, it looks like some fancy hotel back in New York."

Vigeant nodded vigorously, his mouth crammed full of lamb. Then he whispered, "Yeah, but I don't give a damn what the place looks like, the food is great!"

After dinner, the Doctor and his young guests retired to the parlor, where a ceremony of sorts seemed about to take place. Doctor Casey in a grandiose gesture produced a box and offered the sailors cigars from it, along with small glasses of whiskey. The crewmembers were happy to accept such generosity.

"Well gentleman, I want to toast to your success, and your good fortune for having been rescued from the sea down in Ailleabreach. We, the people of Clifden, feel privileged to have been able to help you in any small way.

"Here's to your health, and God bless and grant mercy to your mates who were not able to complete your journey. *Slainte.*"

Doctor Casey lifted his glass, the amber color of the whiskey glowing and shimmering for just a moment in the light from the soft parlor lamp. The lads lifted their glasses unanimously, but not without a collective lump in their throats at the thought of their fallen friends.

Trudeau, standing slightly behind the group, had a hard time controlling his emotions.

"There but for the grace of God," thought the Lieutenant, "go I and the rest of my crew." Trudeau knew he had done as much for his men as he could, but the pain, the grief of loss for a moment threatened to overcome him.

After a moment he spoke.

"Doctor Casey, on behalf of the survivors of the *Damnyankee*, I wish to thank you profoundly for the extreme kindness you have shown us, since the moment you began to care for us on the beach. I can assure you, none of us will ever forget what you have done for us. You have truly been a friend."

Doctor Casey flushed red around his cheeks.

"Well Lieutenant, it's nothing that you would not have done for any of us, had the tables been turned. War is an awful...a terrible thing. I am genuinely pleased to have had even the slightest opportunity to help you. It's nothing that any of you wouldn't have done for us as well," he repeated.

"Doctor, what will happen to us now?" It was Wilbur Lyle.

Casey looked briefly at Trudeau before he spoke. "Well gentlemen, I can't say for sure, but it's my feeling that in the very immediate future you will be leaving Clifden. The Irish government as you know, is neutral in this war, and my guess, and that's all it is at this point, is that in very short order, the government will do whatever it can to get you out of Ireland and back in the hands of your own people, as soon a possible. I can tell you, as soon as I hear anything; I'll relate the news immediately to Lieutenant Trudeau. Now, I think perhaps, I'd best be getting you back to your quarters. It was a splendid evening, wasn't it?"

Once more the crewmembers piled into the back of the small Ford, this time in even better spirits. The car bounced down the road, heavily overloaded. As they began the climb up the hill to the hospital, it began to slow down considerably, lurching a bit from side to side.

"Oh lads, I'm afraid we might be carrying a few stones too many for my dear old Ford," the doctor said. "Would you be offended if I asked a few of you to jump out and walk the rest of the way up the hill, so I can give the old girl a bit of a breather?"

The whole crew tumbled out of the old Ford, and once again thanked the doctor for the wonderful evening, and helped push the old Ford to get it rolling once again, this time homeward. Then they walked the rest of the distance up to the hospital.

The next morning, after they had eaten breakfast, the crewmen sat on the steps of the hospital enjoying a smoke, and watching the morning mist burn off. A sunny day was promised ahead. Olive Harley came around the corner, obviously on her way to visit them.

"Well now Olive, and aren't you a sight for sore eyes," said Frank Cicero, standing up along with the rest of the aviators. They were all already fond of Olive. She had visited them several times, always with a few cigarettes, or a sweet or two.

"Would you like to come in and visit for a bit, Olive?"

"Yes, oh yes I would boys, but not for long. I've got a few more cigarettes for you, and I'd like to ask a favor"

Once they entered the small lounge area of the hospital, which they had commandeered as a gathering place, Vigeant turned to the young Irish woman.

"Now Olive, you've been just great to us. What is it you wanted? If we can do anything for you, just tell us."

She hesitated, a telltale blush rising from her chin all the way to her cheeks.

"Well now, now I've done it for sure, and don't I feel embarrassed to even ask you this silly little favor?"

Trudeau rose from his chair and began to move towards her, eager to make her feel at ease.

"Olive, you are probably our favorite person here in Clifden, so for God's sake, what is it we might be able to do for you?"

"Well Jim… it's just that… I've grown rather fond of the five of you Yanks, and I wondered if… would you mind possibly signing my autograph book, so I'll have a memory of you all, after you leave here?"

"Olive, we would consider it the highest privilege, and a true honor that you would even think of asking us to do this," the Lieutenant said, gently laying his hand on her arm.

Olive hurriedly plunged her hand into the bag she carried, and came out with the autograph book.

"Here Olive, can I be the first to sign your book?"

Jerry Flecker signed it.

Next came Wilbur Lyle, Jim Trudeau, Frank Cicero and Eddie Vigeant. By the time they were done, Olive was once again relaxed, and happy that her wish had been granted.

"Well now, that was grand, and I thank you lads. I'll be able to keep this as a memento, and will always remember this day. It's my hope that I'll see you all once again."

"Olive, you're the best thing ever to come out of Ireland," said Vigeant, and the sudden chorus of "here, here" from the Americans once again brought color to the cheeks of the girl from Clifden.

CHAPTER XVII

LEAVING CLIFDEN, BUT FOR WHERE?

At 1300 hours that day, a Mr. Boyle from the U.S. Legation in Belfast crossed the border at Belcoo, County Fermanagh in his Vauxhall, headed towards Clifden. Unbeknownst to the crew of the *Damnyankee*, the gears for processing their departure from Ireland had already begun to grind.

Later that afternoon Doctor Casey arrived at the hospital in the company of the same Mr. Boyle. Casey asked if he could see Trudeau, and when the Lieutenant appeared in a few minutes, he introduced him to Boyle.

Boyle stuck out his hand in a professional, but not particularly friendly gesture.

"Lieutenant, I am from the American Embassy in Belfast, Northern Ireland. I am here to inform you that we will be removing you and your crew from Ireland. First I would like to briefly interview each of your crewmembers. There are five of you, am I not correct?"

For some reason Trudeau took an instant dislike to this stuffy little man. The civilian official seemed self-important, arrogant, and unsympathetic to what the *Damnyankee* crew had endured.

"Yes, there are five of us left, you're right. But why do you need to interview my men? Also, where are you taking us?"

"Lieutenant, due to security purposes I am not prepared to tell you at this point where you are going. I can say you will be in good hands, and Doctor Casey has agreed that all members of the crew will be fit for travel the day after tomorrow. Now can you arrange for me to take a brief statement from each of your crewmembers, one at a time?"

Trudeau was on the verge of losing his temper when he was pre-empted by Boyle: "Look, Lieutenant, I know this has been difficult on you…on all of you, so I will do my level best to keep these statements as brief and simple as possible."

"Very well, I'll get a small room where you can speak with each of my guys, one at a time. Give me a couple of minutes to arrange a place with the sisters."

The interviews took about an hour for the entire crew. Then Boyle took leave of Trudeau, and told him he'd see him on Wednesday.

"Hey Skipper, what's with the little guy who looked and acted like an undertaker?"

Trudeau looked at Eddie Vigeant and shrugged.

"Eddie, hell if I know. I suppose he's just doing his job, but he wasn't absolutely loaded with personality now, was he?"

Eddie laughed, and then became serious. "Well Skip, at least it sounds like we're on our way to goin' home, but God knows how and when we'll actually get there."

Early on Wednesday morning, another group of officials from the American Embassy arrived at the Clifden Cottage Hospital. The man in charge was a Commodore Easton.

"Lieutenant Trudeau, here, sir." The lieutenant snapped to attention, saluting.

"At ease lieutenant." Easton gave a half salute back.

"Today is the day we are to start you on your journey home. I trust this will meet with your approval?"

"Yessir, I believe every man in my command is ready to leave here, sir. May I ask you where we are headed for, initially?"

"I'm sorry, Lieutenant. Due to the sensitivity of this particular situation I am unable to discuss it with you at the moment. Please believe me when I tell you that you will be safe, and that we will eventually get you back to the States, most likely for reassignment, as soon as we determine your fitness.

"May I ask you to have the men ready to depart no later than 1000 hours? You will embark in an ambulance, which will be waiting for you at the rear entrance to the hospital." Easton whirled about, not waiting for a salute, and strode out the door.

The Commodore seemed like a decent sort, Trudeau thought, but was no more forthcoming with information than Boyle had been. He had no more time to worry about the need for secrecy; the men needed to get ready to leave.

"Gentlemen, listen up. We are going to be leaving Clifden shortly. The destination is confidential. We've enjoyed wonderful hospitality from the people of this town and this whole area. They've been more than good to us, and have brought us much more than we need to take along. What do you think if we get a couple of boxes from the dispensary, so we can have Olive distribute the extra to either school children, or other needy folks?"

Vigeant took charge.

"Skipper, that's a great idea. Okay guys, Jerry, you get the boxes. Let's use one for sweets and stuff the kids might like, and the other for the older folks, who may be hurting for some of the necessities. How much time we got?"

"We'd better hop to, Eddie. We have to be ready no later than 1000 hours."

The crew members immediately dispersed, busying themselves with policing their areas, packing up what little they decided to take, and making the rounds to say brief goodbyes to the people who had cared for them over the last few days.

Trudeau smiled as he watched them. This was one helluva solid group of guys, he thought, and he hoped that he could make whatever lay in store for them a whole lot easier than the last week had been.

The *Damnyankee* survivors greatly appreciated the treatment they had received in Clifden. The local Red Cross had put out an appeal about their situation, undoubtedly with Olive's guidance, and they had been given clothing, candy, razors, combs, toothbrushes, money and even hot-house tomatoes. What was particularly touching was the fact that these gifts came from folks who were struggling themselves to stay afloat. Once boxes had been appropriated, the fellows began to fill them with most of what they had received. Then Frank Cicero pulled his wallet from the back pocket of his dungarees.

"Hey guys, I gotta few bucks, and God knows when I'll be able to spend them. How about those of us who can add a couple of old U. S. of A. greenbacks to the kitty? Y'know damned well these folks can use them, even if they are a bit waterlogged."

He plopped a few bucks into the box for the adults, followed in suit by several crew mates.

At precisely 1003 hours, Commandant Power of the Irish Army came in, accompanied by Captain Robins and Lieutenant Waples from the U.S. Embassy.

"Good morning, Lieutenant Trudeau. I see that you and your men are prepared for the next leg of your journey. I can assure you we will make it as comfortable as possible."

Trudeau returned the greeting, and began to shepherd his crew toward the hospital's entrance. A stickler for promptness, Trudeau made sure the crew had already bid their farewells to the members of the hospital staff. As he squinted in the sunlight of the upper parking lot, Trudeau saw several official-looking automobiles lined up behind a large Irish ambulance.

CHAPTER XVIII

BEHIND THE SCENES

Unbeknownst to the *Damnyankee* survivors, Captain Burthistle, the man who seemed to be in charge of Henry Beckwith's memorial and his body's removal from Clifden, had been busy over the last few days.

First he arranged the transfer of Beckwith's body to the proper British authorities at the border of Northern Ireland. Burthistle had a clandestine contact in the form of a Mrs. Briggs, the wife of the Royal Ulster Constable in the little village of Belleek in the Northern Ireland border county of Fermanagh.

Because of Ireland's stated neutrality, the connection between Burthistle of the Irish Army and the civilian woman was strictly unofficial. It was, however, a vital link in making it possible for the Irish to hand over American and British military men---either alive or dead---to the proper authorities, without causing diplomatic problems over any potential Geneva Convention violations.

They had established a code to indicate a transfer was needed.

"Hallo, Mrs. Briggs, how are you today? This is Burthistle. You know, I'm going to be in the area tonight, and I would love to see your husband, if at all possible. Yes, you think that could be arranged? Very well. Yes, tell him we'll meet for dinner at the usual place. Yes, tell him I'm very much looking forward to seeing him again."

They had worked this out in the early years of the war. A phone call such as this could mean only one thing to Constable Briggs. Burthistle would be delivering either American or British personnel to the usual place, the Royal Hotel, just across the border in Ballyshannon. What Briggs never knew until the actual meeting was whether the transfer would be of those dead or alive.

It was a grisly business, but necessary.

After an uneventful ride north from Clifden through the western Ireland towns of Westport, Castlebar, Ballina and Sligo, the black

Irish ambulance containing the body of Henry Beckwith arrived at the tiny border town of Belleek in the late afternoon.

Burthistle had planned well in advance, and an Irish Army Guard of Honor had been formed from the 17th Infantry Battalion. The guard consisted of a single officer, a bugler, and sixteen soldiers of varying rank. Accompanying Constable Briggs was an American Naval officer.

"Captain Burthistle, it's good to see you, sir." Constable Briggs extended his hand in a formal but friendly handshake.

Burthistle took the hand of his co-conspirator.

"Well Briggs, it's good to see you as well. Perhaps there will come a time when we can greet each other in better circumstances than the present. Pray God that day won't be long in coming."

"Aye Captain, I share your sentiments. 'Tis a rough business, this war. Allow me to introduce you to Captain Robins of the U.S. Navy. He is representing the American forces, and has come to claim his countryman."

Robins stepped forward. He shook Burthistle's extended hand.

"Captain, let me thank you for your efforts to deliver to us one of our own. I know this is not an easy mission for you, and I want to extend to you and all the Irish people the full thanks of America for helping us recover one of our lost sailors.'

The men stepped to the side of the oaken coffin, which had been unloaded from the lorry and placed on a stand by a waiting British Army vehicle. The Irish Army men stood alongside the coffin; a small handful of British soldiers and Royal Ulster Constables lined up on the other side, with Captain Robins amongst them.

The bugler played taps. Then the R.U.C. men loaded the coffin into their lorry. Following a final set of handshakes, they departed eastward, toward Belfast, Northern Ireland's largest city.

The entire ceremony was completed by 1900 hours. Burthistle walked back to his ambulance as the sun began to set over Donegal Bay. He nodded to his driver, and they began the return trip to Athlone.

Burthistle's next task would be to make arrangements for the survivors to make the same trip.

Thus, in the next few days, he once more placed a call to Mrs. Briggs. This time he left the message that he would be traveling through Belleek with five of his family members, and he wondered if Constable Briggs might meet him at the Royal Hotel for lunch. They would have to stop for lunch on any account, and it would at least allow the two friends to visit for a short time. Mrs. Briggs assured Burthistle that she would pass the message on to the Constable, and that he would arrange his schedule so he could spend some time with the Captain.

The Constable's wife immediately went about locating her husband, to pass all this information on to him. My word, she thought; five men would be the largest group they had yet received!

In the meantime, the American Embassy officials, with Commodore Easton in the lead, crossed the border at Belcoo, west of Enniskillen, on their way to Clifden Cottage Hospital from Belfast. They stopped in Castlebar to refuel and add a bit of oil to the engine of the unmarked car.

Lieutenant Waples, the officer driving, was soon busily engaged in conversation with the petrol station attendant. After some time he returned to the car and slid in, behind the wheel.

"What's the matter? You look a bit flummoxed," asked Captain Robins, the other man in the sedan.

"Good God, Captain. You ask these guys what time it is, and they tell you how to build a bleedin' watch! I tried to get directions from this fellow to Clifden, and damned if he didn't proceed to give me about three different routes. Best I can figure, we can go through a place called Ballinrobe, or another place called Claremorris, or yet another place called Westport.

"I've got a mind to just start driving, and whichever sign we see first, that'll be the road we take. I thought the roads were tight enough around Belfast, but these babies make them look like Fifth Avenue!"

As it turned out, they did take a wrong turn, which wasn't difficult to do. They finally pulled into Galway that evening, tired and in poor sorts. They stayed at the Railway Hotel, had a late, uninspired meal, and went to bed.

Even though the trio was running slightly behind schedule, due to that day's mix-up, they left Galway in the morning and headed for Clifden, with better directions than they'd received a day earlier to meet Trudeau and the *Damnyankee* crew.

To transport the Americans, a large, black ambulance was dispatched from St. Enda's Hospital in Salthill, a suburb of Galway.

Declan O'Boyle drove the unwieldy black vehicle. The only other man in the ambulance was young Jimmy Breen, recently assigned as Declan's assistant.

"Well Jimmy, I don't know quite what we've got in store for us today, I don't. I was told to take this old wreck up to Clifden, to the hospital, and that we were going to be taking some American military men north, to the border."

"Jaysus Declan, is it prisoners they are?" Jimmy Breen was a young lad, and had only recently obtained the job as assistant to Declan. "Are these ones criminal, or something?"

"Of course not. Now Jimmy, I'm not sure, but I think they may have been hurt in the war. They didn't tell me much at the hospital, but it should be interesting, and it beats the bejaysus out of the everyday drivin' to and fro from the hospital with some old geezer now, doesn't it? Besides, it looks like it has the makins' of a grand day, and the trip up through Connemara should be a fine one now, shouldn't it?"

"Declan, is that why Doctor Dwyer and Sister Bolton are followin' us in the Doctor's Vauxhall?"

"Aye Jimmy, now you've got the idea. You don't think they'd let us go on a trip like this alone if it was anything of importance now, would ye?"

CHAPTER XIX

THE NORTH OF IRELAND

"For God's sake, the windows are blacked out! How in hell will we know where we're going?"

Trudeau turned in irritation towards Commandant Powers as they walked toward the cars.

"Now Lieutenant, just relax. Our regulations require them, and it may very well be for your own protection."

So that's how it would be.

Trudeau resisted asking Power whether they would be handcuffed for the ride. He thought he'd best save any fit he might want to throw for whatever might transpire down the line.

The ambulance was fitted out with six seats for this trip, which would make the conveyance snug for the Americans. As each crewmember had his own ditty bag, Trudeau asked if the bags could be stored in one of the other cars.

Power pulled Trudeau aside before the American could enter the ambulance after his last crewmember had boarded.

"Listen Lieutenant, I know this is a bit tough on you and your men, but please understand, we aren't doing the black-out to offend or discomfort you. It is a regulation, and much of this has to do with our official position of neutrality. It's better for the Irish government if you aren't observed being hauled around by our Army. I hope you can understand our position here."

Trudeau felt a little better with this explanation.

"Commandant, thanks for taking the time to tell me that. We appreciate all you've done for us. It's a crazy world right now, isn't it? At any rate, best of luck to you, and I'm guessing you'd like to get this show on the road."

They shook hands, this time with meaning. Trudeau turned and climbed into the back of the ambulance.

The gearbox clashed a bit, and the odd procession rolled slowly out of the hospital parking area.

"Skipper, where are we going and what is with the black windows and all the secrecy?" Eddie Vigeant, as usual, wanted to know the wheres and whys of just about everything and anything.

"Eddie, I don't know more than you do. I think the window security may have something to do with Irish neutrality, or the Geneva Convention, or some damned thing like that. Power was pretty decent just before I hopped into this rolling hearse, so I'd think we have little to worry about. Like all of you, I would love to be able to see where in hell we are headed, but that just might not be in the cards. We're certainly going to be turned over to American forces, which is what we all want. Whether we are going to the border of Northern Ireland, or being put on a ship or a plane somewhere, I just don't know." The answer seemed to satisfy Vigeant and the rest of the crew.

Along the way, every time they entered a town, Lieutenant Waples, who was riding in the back with the survivors, pulled down the blackout shades, raising them again when they reentered the countryside. This put the crew more at ease; perhaps the precautions really did relate to the Irish government, and were not designed to harass the crew.

The men of the *Damnyankee* were not advised of either their destination or the route taken, but they watched for road signs when the blackout curtains were raised. The convoy wound itself northeast along the narrow Connemara roads, through Leenane, Westport and Castlebar, tracing the same route the body of Henry Beckwith had followed a few days earlier. They stopped in the market town of Ballina, County Sligo, at the foot of Killala Bay, for supper.

The caravan pulled up at the Hotel Ballina. After a moment, the back door of the ambulance opened, and escorts and crew entered. The Americans ate with great relish.

Cicero started the dinner conversation.

"Migod Wilbur, I don't think I've ever seen you quite this quiet. Look at this man eat."

There were a few chuckles; Lyle was known as a man of few words. He looked up for a moment, smiled, and returned to his plate.

Vigeant just had to be involved whenever there was some ribbing going on.

"For Gods' sake, Wilbur is going to lose his girlish figure. Look at that boy chow down."

Lyle looked up again, slowly put his fork down, and looked at Vigeant.

"Eddie, why am I not surprised that you'd have something to say? Is it just possible that the two of you could allow a poor man a bit of peace over his meal?"

After they ate, the crew sat for a few minutes, some of them enjoying a smoke. Waples soon rose, dropped his napkin on the table, and said, "Well gentlemen, we need to mount up again, as we have more than a few miles to go."

Waples and Robins first surveyed the streets of Ballina. The men were then led out into the afternoon to get back into the ambulance. Once they were out of the town, the shades went up once more. The convoy drummed on, passing through Ballyshannon, then turning easterly toward Beleek.

At around 1600 hours, the convoy pulled off into a small roadside park. They'd reached the border of Northern Ireland. There was no formal ceremony for the survivors.

The *Damnyankee* crew was now the responsibility of the American authorities. The men said goodbye to their Irish escorts, and were quickly loaded into several vehicles at the direction of Waples and Robins.

"Hey Lieutenant Waples, how come there's no blackout curtains?"

"Well, Mr. Vigeant, we are now in Northern Ireland and no longer in a neutral country."

By now it was nearly dark. Before long the two lorries switched on their headlights and eventually pulled over, at Captain Robins' request.

"Gentleman, we are going to stay the night here. It's a small barracks, used by the Royal Ulster Constables. It's not very comfortable, I regret to say, but it's the best we could do for tonight.

"Grab your ditty bags. We'll be out of here early in the morning."

They began to move towards the door of the decrepit-looking Quonset hut.

As they entered the building, in the faint light of a single overhanging bulb, they could see the outlines of a number of bunk beds, with small pillows and rough-looking blankets.

"Gentlemen, I know this isn't the finest place you'll ever bed down in, but I needn't remind you, it's better than the dingy you spent two nights in, and we'll be out of here in the morning. There is a head, but it's outside, around the corner about ten or twelve yards." With that, Robins turned on his heels and was out the door.

The men grumbled a bit as they inspected their new quarters.

"Yeah, well I wonder where he's stayin'; probably the Waldorf friggin' Astoria."

"Okay Eddie, let's zip it up for now." Trudeau approached one of the bunks, unfolded and arranged the blanket, and then began to undress.

"Fellas, this is just one more pit stop on the way home. Now let's suck it up and get some sleep, for whatever the morning brings. We are lucky to be alive, and bad as this is, like Robins said, it's a helluva lot better than that dinghy."

A bit later, Flecker leaned out over his bunk towards Frank Cicero and whispered, "Hey Frankie, I overheard Robins asking the Skipper if he wouldn't prefer to stay with him and Waples at a small hotel. I think he said it was in a place called Fivemiletown. I heard Trudeau tell him he'd just as soon stay with his guys. Think he's gone 'round the bend on us?"

"No Jerry, I don't. Skipper is the kind of guy who'd rather stay with his crew. He doesn't think he's one blinkin' bit better than any of us, and I think we're pretty lucky to have him. That's what I think. You saw some of those other officers during training…hell, they looked like they'd die of fright if they ever had to sit down with us lowly enlisted men. Now shut the hell up, and let me try to get some sleep."

Long after they'd fallen asleep, the crew was awakened by the sound of doors banging, and cursing and shouting from the other side. Some other men had come into the other end of the Quonset hut, and by the sound of it, they were much the worse for wear after a night of carousing.

"Good God. I hope these R.U.C. guys, or whoever they are, can fight one helluva lot better than they can drink."

Eventually the ruckus died down, and the *Damnyankee* crewmen settled back to sleep as well as they could, wondering what the morning would bring.

CHAPTER XX

OFF TO ENGLAND

Early the next morning, Waples returned.

"Gentlemen, it appears you survived the night. Be prepared to mount up in about fifteen minutes, and we will be on our way. We'll stop for breakfast in about half an hour. Please return your bunks into the same condition you found them in."

In spite of their sleep being interrupted by the midnight revelers, the men were in high spirits.

"If it were up to me, I'd drop mine in the nearest lake. I think the concrete floor might have been softer."

"Oh Eddie, for God sakes, you'd complain if they hung you with a new rope," said Cicero.

"OK ladies, let's can the conversation and get ready to evacuate this dump. Don't know about you, but I could eat half a cow."

Trudeau, anxious to get on with the journey, was hungrier than he had been since the ditching.

This time they were loaded into three different cars. The caravan headed east by northeast towards Belfast. Once there, they were taken to a military hospital on the city's outskirts, where they were to remain for almost ten days.

Their treatment in Northern Ireland was in stark contrast to what they encountered in Clifden. They were required to remain in their ward, not even being permitted to walk the halls and corridors of the hospital. Few people spoke with them at all. Trudeau, due to his status as the group's only officer, was taken to a special section of the hospital with a private room. He protested about being separated from his men, and was finally allowed to rejoin them.

Eventually they were told by a hospital official that they were going to be removed from the hospital the following morning. Around mid-day on October 1, 1944, the five survivors were taken to a military airfield in the outskirts of Belfast, and were loaded onto a U.S. Navy Catalina seaplane. This was the same type of craft

Trudeau had been flying in Florida, prior to his assignment to the program that eventually led to his command of the *Damnyankee.*

It was a short hop to London. Trudeau was immediately separated from the enlisted men, and taken to the Reindeer Club in Soho, where he would be domiciled. Although befitting a commissioned naval officer, the young lieutenant would have preferred to be allowed to stay with his crew. He was told the men would be billeted at the local YMCA.

An American naval officer gave Trudeau a uniform replacement allowance. He was directed towards Selfridge's, a very fine London department store, where he ordered a hand-tailored replacement uniform, which would be ready the following day. Trudeau felt good about this opportunity, because his clothes were tattered and worn. He also thought that having the customarily sharp military appearance would go some distance towards restoring his own image, and that this would help his crew in restoring their own confidence and military sense of bearing, as well.

Trudeau returned to the Reindeer Club, to find that all of his personal belongings, such as they were, consisting mainly of toiletries given him by the generous people of Clifden, were missing. He knew a number of 8th Army Air Corps pilots were also bunking there. So much for honor amongst fellow officers, Trudeau thought.

Oh well. Better to concentrate on what really mattered: the enlisted men.

The concierge gave him directions to the YMCA club, and he set off in search of the crew. He wanted to make sure they were going to be properly cared for on their first night in England.

Earlier, the other *Damnyankee* survivors had been unceremoniously dropped off and told they could find billets in a local YMCA in the area. None of the men knew where they were, as it was the first visit to London for all. The directions they were given were confusing, and they spent several hours wandering the streets of war-torn London. Hearing music coming from a bar, they'd gone in, to find a number of R.A.F. fighter pilots inside; one of whom was playing a piano in the corner. The young Americans were completely ignored, so they decided to take their chances back out on the street. Understandably, the *Damnyankee* crew was becoming anxious as to where they would sleep.

"Excuse me, pal," Vigeant asked one formal-looking stranger. "Can you please tell me where in heck the heart of this city is? We're looking for the center of London. We're supposed to find a place called the Young Men's Christian Association."

The fellow seemed to be taking visual inventory of the group. In a not-altogether-approving manner, he pointed in an easterly direction with his walking stick, and said quite solemnly, "You cawn't miss it...it's that way."

After the fellow continued on his way, Vigeant looked at Cicero and said,

"See Frankie, I told you...you really *cawn't* miss the bloody place!"

The others followed Vigeant's lead in the direction indicated, the young aviator swinging an imaginary umbrella, in imitation of the Brit.

They hunted some more for the YMCA, and finally came upon it. The YMCA attendant inside the lobby, however, told the travelers there was no space available for them there. The men were unenthusiastically directed to a place called the Moster Club to find a place to stay.

They found the nearby Moster Club fairly easily. It was managed by a man who was also named Power.

"For Chrissakes, is there *no other* name in our future other than Power?" Vigeant muttered.

Mr. Power at the Moster Club was not receptive to their inquiries either, as it also had no empty rooms. Trudeau found the dispirited group of sailors chatting outside about what next to try. After hearing their story during the improvised curbside conference, he resolved to help find lodging for his men.

"Okay fellas, listen up. We're going to go back to the YMCA, and I'll persuade 'em. They owe it to us to let you stay there. Hell, if it weren't for guys like you, the Brits would never have recovered from Dunkirk. I'll try to be more diplomatic than that, and I'm hoping he'll get the general drift of it. You're not sleeping on the streets."

Trudeau engaged the YMCA desk clerk in an earnest conversation while the men waited outside. He assured the man that, as an American officer, he had been told specifically by British military authorities that his crew was to be billeted in the YMCA. He began to wear down the clerk with his polite insistence, and a militaristic show of resolve. The clerk finally said the men could stay there.

Trudeau thanked the clerk, went back out to the street, and told his crewmen they had a place to sleep. After a long, tiring day, they welcomed the news with lightened spirit.

Once he saw his men safely ensconced in the YMCA, Trudeau was ready to depart for his own quarters at the Reindeer Club.

"Fellas, I've got some paperwork to do tomorrow, and am scheduled to get a new uniform later in the day. Rest up. I'll get my stuff out of the way, and then we will begin to try to figure out how we will get out of here and on our way back home."

"Skipper, if you can do anything to get us on the way home, I'm all on your side, and I'm sure the fellas will be as well."

"Thanks Frank. I think before long we are going to look back on this weird journey and wonder how things happened the way they did. With all we've been through, I'm sure we'll be able to handle the rest of this. I've got a feeling that I'm gonna get a chokehold on this craziness tomorrow, once and for all. I'll see all of you the next day. Take it easy and rest up a bit. Goodnight."

"Goodnight, Skipper."

"Thanks, Skipper, for getting a place for us to bed down in."

The men paid a nominal sum for lodging from the monies they'd received from the Navy upon entering England. Then they were led to a couple of rooms with old metal bunks lining the walls in every possible spot.

"Hey Frankie, this place ain't much, but compared to sleepin' on the sidewalk, I feel like it's the Waldorf."

Flecker tried to bounce on a lower bunk, but there wasn't much spring left in the tired old coils beneath the thin mattress. Exhausted from the day in a strange and unfriendly city, the young Americans fell asleep almost instantly.

Their heads seemed to have hardly hit the pillows when the screeching and clanging of a Klaxon horn began somewhere.

"Good God, what now?"

"What the hell is this?"

The door to the bunk room opened, and the clerk yelled, "It's an air raid. Get dressed right this minute. I'll lead you to the shelter."

The *Damnyankee's* crew was already up, grumbling and cussing as they searched for shoes and trousers. The room's lights were on, but the blackout curtains were firmly in place over all the windows. They stumbled down the stairway, following the night-clerk-turned-air-warden down the darkened street less than a block, and then hurried down an outside staircase and through a metal door.

Dozens of Londoners were already inside, and dozens more came in after them, with little sign of concern, or even interest.

"Damn Jerry, will you look at these folks? It's like this is no big deal…seems like they do this every day. Some of them look like they're practically sleepwalking."

"You know Frank; it might just be that these people go through the same thing almost every night. Did you see all of the bombed-out buildings since we hit this burg?"

They could hear muffled sounds in the distance.

"The bloody Jerry bastards aren't that close now tonight, are they?" murmured an elderly lady, standing by herself, with a scarf around her head, to nobody in particular.

Her simple statement had no need of an answer. After about an hour, another, mellower bell rang throughout the shelter.

"Okay lads, the danger is over for now. It's back to sleep if you'd like." Out of nowhere the clerk reappeared and began to herd the now wide-awake crew back to the YMCA. As they walked through the darkened streets of London, they could see an orange glow on the horizon to the west of them.

"Hey Jerry, check out the fires off there in the distance. These poor guys must get hit like this almost every night. This has gotta happen all the time. No wonder they practically sleepwalked into the shelter."

"Yeah Eddie, this place didn't get this torn up like this by accident, did it?"

The men muttered about their less-than-expected quarters as they readied again for bed.

"Why in hell did they bring us over here to London, and make no arrangements for us to stay anywhere? Are we in trouble for something? It's almost like they want to forget that we exist. This is unfair. Aren't there any American military men who care what happens to us?"

The same thoughts were running through Trudeau's mind that night. He willed himself to sleep, knowing he needed rest if he were going to be able to look after his crew. His last thought had something to do with having brought them this far, he would just dig in and get them home.

Trudeau awakened the following morning somewhat restored, with additional resolve to improve the morale of the crew of the *Damnyankee*, as well as find a way to re-establish their status as American military personnel.

Over a first cup of coffee at the Reindeer Club, he began to formulate the day's plan of action. Lieutenant Jackson, an 8th Army pilot whom Trudeau had met briefly the day before, slid onto the bench across the table.

"Good mornin', Skipper. And how do you feel after a good night's sleep?"

"Good morning, Joe. I'm feeling a bit better."

Trudeau had developed an instant liking for the Army aviator.

"I've been working out a way in my head to get over this 'Men from no country' situation, and to get back in control of the immediate future. I'm worried about my crew. These lads have been through way too much to be treated like this."

"Well Jim, from the little I know of you, I get the feeling that you'll get this whole thing sorted out pronto."

The second day in London, Trudeau picked up his uniform and explored various avenues to get his crew home. Meanwhile, his enlisted crewmembers were taken to a U.S. military quartermaster location, where they were also given new uniforms, and $25 cash each.

CHAPTER XXI

ADVENTURES IN LONDON, THEN HOMEWARD BOUND

Buoyed by the night at the YMCA, new togs, and some jingle in their pockets, the ever-resilient *Damnyankee* crew set out to see a bit of London. After several hours, they found themselves in a neighborhood with a number of pubs.

"Hey guys, this looks like the London I'd like to see. Check it out…I'm gonna go over and see what's going on with this lovely young lady."

Cicero sauntered across the street towards a woman who appeared to be dawdling along. She stepped seductively from foot to foot in a tantalizing strut, her big eyes watching the young American approaching her.

"Hey baby, how's about a cigarette?" Cicero reached into his blouse and extracted a pack of Camels, cracking it on the top of his hand, causing one of the cigarettes to pop up. The woman took it, dangled it from her ruby red lips, awaiting Cicero's flick of his Zippo lighter. Then she bent over the flame, took a deep drag, and blew the resultant smoke slowly out her nostrils. Cicero was encouraged by all of this.

"Wanna get a drink with me?"

"Well Yank, I might like to do a lot more with you than just having a drink. How much money you got on you? We could get really friendly!"

This was not the kind of action he was hoping for. Cicero, realizing what he'd wandered into, paled, then blurted out, "Yeah…well gee, I'd like to hang around a bit, but I guess I've gotta get back to my buddies!"

Back in the safety of his crewmates, he tried to cover what he knew was an embarrassing blush, while trying to appear in control of the situation.

"Hey Frankie…hey lover boy, what happened? How come you're back here so quick?"

"Shut up Jerry…just can it, Okay?"

That was the extent of the *Damnyankee* crew's involvement with London's ladies of the night.

The next day the men were once again ambling around London, and came upon a zoo. After fast-talking their way through the admitting gate, no doubt helped along in this endeavor by their American Navy uniforms, they came upon a large bull, standing in a paddock.

"Hey guys, look at this fella!"

Cicero, posed like a matador, approached the paddock with a certain rhythm in his step, affecting what he thought to be the arrogant swagger of a Spanish bullfighter. "Ole…Toro…watch me bring this beast to his knees!"

Cicero reached through the paddock slats, and grabbed the bull by both horns. Immediately the slobbering beast turned wild-eyed, and with a single twist of his massive neck, threw the young sailor up against the side of the paddock. Cicero winced with pain, holding his left arm gingerly. The bull ignored his would-be tormentor, dug his hoof in the dirt, shook his magnificent head, and walked away from the side of the paddock.

"Hey Frankie…want to show us that move again…. Toro, Toro, eh hombre? You scared the hell out of that bull, didn't you?"

"Shut up Jerry, okay, just button it up!"

Cicero rubbed his arm as they moved on. And that was the extent of the *Damnyankee* crew's involvement with London's wild animals.

The end of their adventure was clearly in sight.

On October 15th, after two weeks in London, the enlisted crewmen boarded a four-engine aircraft, a British Sunderland, and flew to Belfast, to begin their journey back to the United States.

The hop from London to Belfast was wonderfully uneventful. Even the usually quiet Lyle was relieved to be on their way.

"I don't know about you guys, but the sooner I'm off these ocean-crossing airplanes, the better."

In Belfast they were taken by lorry to another airport to board a Pan-American Clipper ship.

The *Damnyankee* crewmen found themselves traveling in the company of a Navy Admiral on the second plane. Upon meeting the

Admiral and his small entourage, Vigeant was enlisted as a special courier for the return flight. He spent the entire trip with a valise, reportedly full of Top Secret papers, handcuffed to his wrist.

The Admiral was returning from France, where he had amassed an impressive collection of French perfume to take home. During the flight, several of the bottles leaked, due to changes in air pressurization. The cabin's atmosphere grew quite sweet.

"Jeez, Frankie, the inside of this plane is starting to smell like that little tart you talked to on the streets of London."

"Aw c'mon Eddie, are you ever going to cut me some slack? How's about letting up on me...what the hell, we're on our way home now."

It would have taken a good deal more than this kind of banter to get these guys upset.

"I'll tell you what, Frankie. You can bet that I'll be ready to get rid of this blinkin' briefcase by the time we get back to the good old U.S. of A."

Vigeant struggled to find a comfortable way to sit on the plane. He finally arranged a couple of G.I. blankets on the seat next to him, so he could rest the courier valise without it constantly dragging on his arm.

As the westward flight proceeded to cross the North Atlantic, the crew members seemed to lapse into their own private little worlds, reliving the experiences and horrors of their own eastward flight, and the ditching off Ireland. It seemed like an eternity had passed since they first left Norfolk.

The plane landed and refueled in Newfoundland, then worked its way down the northeast coast of North America. It landed without incident at New York's La Guardia Field.

Due to the presence of the Admiral, delays upon embarking were minimal. The Admiral magnanimously announced to the immigration officials that the *Damnyankee* crewmembers were part of his travel contingent. Once through the gate they were stopped briefly by several FBI agents, who quickly relieved Vigeant of the valise he had chained to his wrist.

Vigeant, Cicero and Wilbur Lyle all accompanied Jerry Flecker to his home in Brooklyn, where Jerry's mother treated them to their first home-cooked American meal in quite some time.

143

CHAPTER XXII

TRUDEAU RETURNS HOME

Trudeau returned to America separately, on a direct route to Norfolk, Virginia aboard a four-engine Coronado Flying Boat, owned by Pan American Airlines, on loan to the Navy.

He enjoyed flying on a seaplane once again. He was asked by the pilot if he would like to fly for awhile, and enjoyed it. It was his first time flying a Coronado.

While he had instructed in PBY's, this was his first time flying a Coronado. When Trudeau wasn't in the cockpit, checking things out, he visited with Admiral John Hall Jr., who was also returning stateside.

The Admiral, a 1913 graduate of Annapolis, had been Naval Chief of Staff for the 1942 invasion of Morocco, and commanded the amphibious assault on Normandy's Omaha Beach on D-Day in 1944. He was keenly interested in the story of Trudeau's ditching off the West of Ireland. The junior officer and the wise old veteran of two world wars got along famously.

"Admiral Hall, sir, would you mind doing me a personal favor?" asked Trudeau, as he reached into his back trouser pocket and drew out his well-worn billfold.

"Well Lieutenant, if there's something I can do for you, by all means let's have a go at it."

"Well sir, I've carried this short snorter with me since I've been in the service, and I'd be very pleased if you wouldn't mind signing it for me."

The young pilot had pulled a single dollar bill out of his well-worn billfold and handed it to Admiral. He was carrying on what had become a military tradition that, in the event of meeting someone of importance, you obtained their autograph.

"Lieutenant Trudeau, I am honored that you would be interested in me signing it, and believe me, it's a privilege for me to be able to do so."

The Admiral dutifully signed it, and Trudeau slipped the dollar bill back into his wallet.

The Coronado landed uneventfully in Norfolk, and taxied slowly along the shore. When the pilot finally cut the engines, a crew of young sailors entered the water next to the huge seaplane, hauling floating attachable land wheels. They swam around, working to attach the wheels, then thrashed their way back out of the river. The head of the detail flashed an "all's clear" sign to the cockpit. The pilot acknowledged their work, ran up the two inboard engines, and taxied the seaplane up the ramp, and down the runway.

Trudeau watched these extra steps for securing the seaplane, bade farewell tp the plane's crew, thanking them, and then walked out the hatch and down the ladder.

Like his crew, it felt like it'd been ten years since they'd left Norfolk.

As he tossed his ditty bag over his shoulder and began walking toward the transient hangar, the pilot was in a somber mood, thinking of Carl Snavely, Phil Mills, Joe Fleucher, Vernon Peterson and Henry Beckwith. Such great men, such young men, and he'd never get to see them again. They'd never have the chance to grow up or grow old. He had spent a lot of time over the last weeks pondering what if anything he could have done to help them in the cold water off Ireland. Sad as he was, he kept arriving at the same conclusion…there was nothing more that he and the surviving crewmembers could have done to save the others.

Trudeau was met by a young Ensign, who gestured to a gray U.S. Navy DeSoto sedan parked near the transient hangar.

"Lieutenant, my orders are to take you to the base hospital, as there are still some concerns regarding your health."

Trudeau nodded glumly. He hated to admit it, but he was still having trouble with his stomach.

While in the base hospital, doctors discovered that the young pilot had lost some of his stomach lining, due no doubt to ingesting fuel while bobbing in the Atlantic by the ditched plane.

After his recuperation, Lieutenant Jim Trudeau spent the remainder of his time in the military stationed in Norfolk.

During his recuperation, Trudeau was visited one day by a Major Howard, Army Air Corps, from Washington D.C. Howard had called in advance, asking Trudeau if he would mind meeting with him, as he'd been conducting an extensive study regarding the at-sea ditching of B-24's, and would be most interested in discussing Trudeau's personal experience off the coast of Ireland.

The next day Howard arrived with a second lieutenant in tow. Trudeau noticed that Howard was possessed of a strange facial tick, and every 10 to 20 seconds his head would jerk almost violently to the side. After initial introductions, Howard asked Trudeau a number of questions regarding his experience in setting the *Damnyankee* down in the seas off Ireland. They spoke for almost an hour, when Howard abruptly gestured to his aide, who left the room on some undisclosed mission.

"Lieutenant Trudeau, if you don't mind, I brought with me motion picture film of two separate ditchings involving B-24's, and I'd very much like it if you would review them with me, as your input would be most helpful."

"Major Howard, I'll try to be as helpful as I can. Would you mind telling me how you were able to acquire this footage? Was someone just in the right place at the right time? How could this happen twice?

Howard laughed lightly. "Well Lieutenant, these weren't quite as accidental as was yours. You see, they were staged ditchings, as the Air Corps was looking for any possible recommendations they might use with '24 crews in training, to maximize the possibility of crew survival."

"How in hell did you ever convince these pilots to intentionally ditch one of those big birds. Were they nuts?"

Howard laughed again, but this time with just the slightest edge in his voice. "Well Lieutenant Trudeau, it wasn't all that difficult. You see, I was the pilot in both ditchings."

Trudeau felt thunderstruck, making every attempt not to sound so. "Major Howard, excuse my lack of sensitivity. I'm just astounded that you were able to do that. I don't know I've ever met a man brave enough to have undertaken something like that, particularly twice in a row. I know I've had all I need as far as that experience goes. I'm not looking forward to ever repeating it."

"Well Lieutenant, your experience was on an emergency basis, you were carrying a full crew, and you were in the worst of conditions. My situation was a bit more controlled. It is of course impossible to duplicate the conditions that you ditched your aircraft under. The film that we will be watching shows ditches that I conducted on the Charles River, here in Virginia."

By this time the aide had returned with a cart supporting the bulky 16mm projector, and after a few moments of adjustment, he signaled the Major that he was prepared to roll film.

The whirring and clacking of the projector began, and Trudeau watched intently, as if in a trance. From time to time Howard would signal to have the projector stopped, and they'd rewind the film long enough for him to be able to re-run a sequence, asking Trudeau's opinion about a particular technical question.

Jeezus, thought Trudeau...who in hell would be crazy enough to do this *voluntarily*...and not once, but *twice*?

Major Howard proceeded to tell Trudeau that the Army had filled a number of the in-wing fuel tanks with thousands of ping-pong balls, to increase the flotation capability of the aircraft.

"Lieutenant Trudeau, watch carefully as we run the second ditching for you."

Trudeau had no problem focusing on the screen, and when they ran the ditching of the second B-24, the nose dropped almost imperceptibly into the smooth water of the bay. Getting the nose down just a matter of what looked like inches to Trudeau brought the warplane to such a jolting halt that the horizontal stabilizers ripped right off the plane.

"Major, in one respect, that calm water may be more danger than the open sea. I was able to bounce my plane once, off the top of a wave, and I believe that may have slowed me a bit. When you hit that calm, flat water, it looks like you just nosed into freshly poured concrete."

The conversation went on for a half hour or so, with Howard pausing from time to time to make a brief entry into a well-worn note book. Finally the Major wrapped up the meeting, and his aide began to break down the projector.

"Lieutenant Trudeau, I appreciate you taking the time with me. There are a number of things I learned from you that I may be able to incorporate into my ongoing research."

The men took leave of each other, and Trudeau found himself in his ward, musing over the recently terminated meeting. He felt something seemed odd about the Major, but couldn't quite put his finger on it.

Lieutenant Jim Trudeau spent the remainder of his time in the military stationed in Norfolk, the very place where the *Damnyankee* had departed from, enroute to the European theater. Like so many thousands of other military personnel, Trudeau was released back into the civilian world at the end of the war, in 1945. He continued to have problems with his stomach for a number of years after the war.

Chapter XXIII

COMING BACK TO IRELAND

On September 11, 1994, three days before the fiftieth anniversary of the ditching of the *Damnyankee* off the west coast of Ireland, Jim Trudeau returned to Clifden. With him were his second wife Lyn, and Eddie Vigeant's widow, Dorothy, and a number of family members, including her granddaughter Jennifer.

They came back to participate in the unveiling of a monument to his crew which was built in Ballyconneely at the roadside, not far from where they had washed ashore.

While Trudeau had prepared some words for the occasion, when the time came to talk, he put his notes aside and spoke simply from his heart.

A small but lovely reception was held at the little cottage where Trudeau and Vigeant first found respite from the sea back in 1944. By this time it was owned by Gabriel McNamara, a fisherman and the son of Paddy McNamara, the gentleman who had owned the first house where they had knocked.

At both the cottage, and at the beach where the dinghy had washed up half a century earlier, Trudeau broke down in memory of his crew.

The bronze plaque, set against the stone obelisk, carries an image of a PB4Y-1, with the following inscription:

UNITED STATES NAVY
PB4Y-1 LIBERATOR BOMBER
SERIAL NO. 38799

ENROUTE FROM NAS NORFOLK, VIRGINIA, USA TO
REYKJAVIK, ICELAND, DITCHED OFF THIS COAST
ON 14 SEPTEMBER 1944. AFTER APPROXIMATELY
33 HOURS IN A LIFE-RAFT, THE SURVIVING CREW
MEMBERS CAME ASHORE NEAR THIS SPOT. THEY SPENT
FOUR DAYS IN CLIFDEN HOSPITAL, WHERE THEY WERE
TREATED WITH CARE AND COMPASSION.

THE CREW ROSTER IS AS FOLLOWS:
SURVIVORS
    LT. JAMES O. TRUDEAU – PILOT
    A.G.M. S/C JOSEPH E. VIGEANT – GUNNER
    A.M.M. 2/C WILBER LYLE – GUNNER
    A.R.M. 3/C GERALD FLECKER – GUNNER
    S.1/C FRANK CICERO – GUNNER
KILLED IN ACTION
    S. 1/C HENRY E. BECKWITH – GUNNER
    ENS. PHILLIP MILLS – NAVIGATOR
    ENS. CARL SNAVELY – CO-PILOT
    A.R.M. 2/C JOSEPH FLEUCHER – 1ST RADIO
    A.M.M. 3/C VERNON PETERSON – 2ND MECHANIC

LEST WE FORGET

ERECTED BY THE PEOPLE OF BALLYCONNEELY
& CLIFDEN AND THE WARPLANE RESEARCH GROUP
OF IRELAND -- 11 SEPTEMBER 1994

RESEARCHING THE STORY

Were Jim Trudeau and his crew of nine very young men heroes? That's not for me to say, or even know. There were thousands of men just like them during World War II, taking each challenge one at a time. This was unquestionably the greatest military undertaking in the history of civilization. As with most wars, much of the burden fell upon the shoulders of our youngest men, some of them as much boy as man.

This is just one story in many, one I could not walk away from.

It's been an occasionally frustrating, but mostly pleasant journey from the inception of this book through its completion. This being my first attempt at writing a book, each step was akin to exploring new territory for me. That proved to be both complicated while at the same time strangely freeing, as I, through my lack of knowledge of the process itself, had no pre-set tenets to follow.

Early on I decided, particularly after meeting Jim Trudeau and getting to know him, that I would do my best to tell the story of the *Damnyankee* and its crew in the most forthright and simple manner I could muster. I felt the truths of the story would hold up by themselves, and my job would be to tell of their experiences as honestly as I could.

The seed for this undertaking was first planted on a trip to Ireland in May of 2000, just after moving into our new home outside Driggs, Idaho, in the heart of the Grand Teton range on the Wyoming-Idaho border.

It was our sixth visit to Ireland since 1990, and the first since my retirement the previous year. My wife Wynne Ann and I were driving through County Galway and decided to spend the night in Clifden. We'd stayed there several times on earlier trips, having enjoyed both the town and its reputation as a center for Irish music. After trying a bed and breakfast we'd stayed at a few years earlier and finding it booked, we drove back down the Faul Road a bit and saw a nice B&B named "Failte," the Irish word for welcome.

As we drove through the gate and up the beautifully landscaped drive toward the house, little did I know what lay ahead of me, based on a random selection of a B&B with a lovely driveway.

The proprietors were Sean and Maureen Kelly. Sean was a great conversationalist, and Wynnie has always maintained I could have a meaningful conversation with a stone wall. Well, Sean Kelly is anything but a stone wall, so we had a wonderful talk over tea.

A retired Sergeant in the Garda, he was most interested in my passion for Ireland, and wondered why I returned as often as I did. One thing led to another, and Sean told me, "You know, I'm impressed with your knowledge of and love for Ireland. Not many Americans seem to have the passion for Ireland that you do. I have something that you might well enjoy looking at. I'll be just a minute." With that he got up and left the room, reappearing in a few minutes with a huge three-ring binder, stuffed with papers.

At that moment, I was unaware that Kelly was introducing something into my life that I would not be able to put aside. I had no idea that this would be the beginning of a six-year project for me.

"This contains everything I know about a strange occurrence that happened here back in the mid-80's when an American fellow showed up and told me about an aircraft ditching he had been involved with, back in the war. I found it quite interesting, and spent a bit of time learning about the story. It's my thought that you may find it of interest as well, particularly with your having come here all the way from America. I'll leave it with you, and you are most welcome to look at it in your room."

I thanked Sean, and told him I'd enjoy perusing it. We went out for dinner that evening, and being tired from the day's travel, decided to skip the Irish music in favor of retiring early to the Failte House.

I began paging through Sean's binder, reading, amongst many other items, an account of this historical event published by an organization called the Warplane Research Group of Ireland (WRGI).

I was later to find that WRGI consisted primarily of two Irish gentlemen, Frank Donaldson and Victor Sullivan, both Corkmen. The more I read, the more I was drawn to the story of this military aircraft incident of so many years prior.

Beyond the WRGI report, Kelly had assembled a fascinating

collection of letters, official documents, and e-mails from many of the principals involved, dating back to 1985. When I took a break, Wynne Ann began to read, at which point we had a minor disagreement as to who was entitled to continue reading.

Having learned over previous trips that the intelligent way to visit Ireland is to travel slowly, we both agreed to extend our stay at the Kelly's another day. This allowed us to amicably settle the discussion of who got to read what.

After breakfast the next morning, Sean and I sat down and discussed the entire *Damnyankee* incident over a cup of coffee.

When he unexpectedly asked me if we'd like to visit the site of the beach landing with him, without even asking Wynnie, I hurriedly answered yes, if it wasn't too much trouble. I knew she'd be as interested as I was. The beaching of the *Damnyankee* crew wasn't the only historical event of aeronautical significance to have happened in this tiny part of Ireland.

Sean drove us down to Ailleabreach, stopping at the Alcock and Brown aviation memorial on the way. This monument, in the form of an airplane wing, celebrated the world's first transatlantic aircraft Crossing: On June 15th, 1919, British aviators Alcock and Brown flew a little more than 1,980 miles in 16 hours and 27 minutes from Newfoundland to just south of Clifden. They landed their Vimy IV World War I aircraft somewhat by accident in the Derrygimla Moor, a bog that wasn't exactly a decent airfield.

After a brief stop, we arrived in Ailleabreach, where Sean took a side road, pulling up at a shoulder high stone obelisk. Here was the monument to the crew of the *Damnyankee*. It was a solemn moment for me. I knew next to nothing about the people who had beached near here almost 56 years earlier.

Sean then drove us further along a narrower road, pulling up alongside the sea, just short of a stone cottage with a thatch roof. It was close by to a more substantial home, and when Sean approached the door of the second house, a woman came out and greeted him.

There we met the wife of Gabriel McNamara, the son of Paddy McNamara, the man Trudeau and Vigeant had first encountered, who hadn't allowed them to enter his home in the night, fearing they were Germans.

Years earlier, the McNamaras had acquired the small cottage, the former home of Michael Conneely, the deceased bachelor who had provided Trudeau and Vigeant their first respite from the sea.

Gabriel's wife was kind enough to fetch the key, and let us into the tiny cottage. The walls were neatly whitewashed, and one wall held framed pictures of Ed Vigeant and Jim Trudeau, both in uniform. On another wall was the small turf fireplace which had warmed their exhausted bodies.

After a brief chat and a couple of photographs, we thanked her for her hospitality and returned to Clifden. It was a profound experience, and made the extra day's stay more than worthwhile.

Upon returning to America, I was never quite able to erase the *Damnyankee* and its crew from my mind. I found myself wondering what Vigeant and Trudeau were really like, and how this incident, relatively early in their lives, had affected them.

A year and a half later, Wynnie and I were talking one evening when the subject of Ailleabreach came up. Somehow the story of a handful of American aviators washing ashore on that lovely but isolated Irish beach stuck in my mind like a bone lodges in your throat. She suggested I write about it.

It was less than two years since we'd met the Kellys, and first heard the story of the *Damnyankee*. I was encouraged upon hearing back from Sean a few weeks after I wrote him, in September, 2001.

Thus began the transition from thinking about the *Damnyankee* and her crew to a tentative initial commitment to doing as much research as I could. I wanted to ferret out the story of these young Americans.

With Sean's assistance, I was able to get in touch with both Frank Donaldson and Victor Sullivan from the Warplane Research Group of Ireland.

Let me put this as plainly as possible: without the help of both Donaldson and Sullivan and their painstaking research, this book would never have seen the light of day.

Also critical---the character and reputation of Sean Kelly. On every occasion where I was looking for assistance on my research, the mere mention of his name opened doors for me, doors that quite possibly would have remained shut, were I left to my own machinations.

Jim Trudeau was by now long retired, and living in Gainesville,

Florida. To my letter of introduction, Trudeau was friendly and most polite, but properly concerned about whom I might be, and what my concerns, motives and qualifications were. Sean Kelly's name--- because Sean had been instrumental in putting together the 1994 monument unveiling---went a long way towards ameliorating Trudeau's concerns about me, as well as my intentions.

"I'll talk to any friend of the Kelly's," Trudeau wrote me by e-mail that October, shortly after his 85th birthday.

Jim Trudeau agreed to meet with me in Florida the following spring, as soon as my ski season was over.

In the interim, we became acquainted with each other. I sent him copies of magazines I had been published in, and we traded e-mails. It soon became apparent I was dealing with a man of excellent intelligence, and a razor-sharp wit. I'd grown to like Trudeau well before we met in person. I would find out he's the kind of guy you could spend two hours with, and it would seem like two minutes. My regret now is that we live so far apart; as I would love to be able to see more of Jim.

Writing a historical novel would obviously have been an easier task. After spending several days with Trudeau and his wife Lyn, however, the integrity of the man convinced me to tell the story as it actually unfolded.

A talented writer on his own accord, Jim contributed immensely to this book. In too many places to enumerate, his input helped me along the way.

At this point, there were only two survivors still living, Jim and his crewman Jerry Flecker. Jerry Flecker didn't particularly want to be involved, as he "prefers to live in the present, and not the past." I spoke with Flecker twice; on both occasions he was able to confirm several facts, and was a very decent guy.

Eddie Vigeant passed away in 1992; he's buried at the Oakwood Cemetery in Troy, New York. Efforts to find the final resting places of the other *Damnyankee* survivors were unsuccessful.

In Florida, Trudeau had arranged for me to meet with Dorothy Vigeant, Eddie's widow, and their granddaughter Jennifer Corona, an attorney. Jennifer had accompanied her grandparents on two separate occasions to Ireland, one being the monument dedication. Dorothy provided additional perspective and details during a pleasant afternoon. She helped flesh out the character of Eddie Vigeant, who by the very force of his personality was a major piece of the puzzle.

On a trip to Ireland in May 2002, we met with Donaldson and Sullivan of the WRGI, and spent more time with Sean and Maureen. We wanted to do some additional research. On the evening we arrived there, we were all so pleased to see each other that precious little was said about the *Damnyankee.* That night I asked Sean if he'd been able to set up any meetings for the following day.

Sean looked at me with utter seriousness, and apologized for not having taken the time to *type out our itinerary* for the following morning! I assured Sean that was not a requirement! His comment should have been an indication of the lengths Sean Kelly had gone to in order to prepare for the following morning. It would turn out to be one of the most memorable days of my life.

We departed for Ailleabreach early. It was a day not fit for men or dogs. The wind and rain were pounding in from the Atlantic. With the weather worsening each mile, we headed south.

Our first stop was Lookout Position 53, where Martin O'Malley had made the phone call advising Clifden that the *Damnyankee* survivors had come ashore. To climb up there, we first had to seek permission from the landowner of the parcel we must go through to reach the lookout. By now the rain was lashing in off the coast in torrential sheets. It was, as the Irish say, a day where it rained uphill. We sat in the car watching Sean make his way to her door. He told her two Americans wanted to go to the top of the hill, and the woman asked, "Are they mad?" When Sean assured her he'd accompany us, she asked again, "And Sean, have ye gone mad yerself?"

Mad we might have appeared. The track up to LOP 53 was steep and slippery. Sean's agility astonished me; he nearly raced up the hill, oblivious to the battering from rain and wind. We struggled to keep up, following a trail of marker stones still in place, their whitewashed "53' markings faded by exposure. Eventually we topped the hill and took refuge from the elements in the post; a windowless concrete pillbox built at the outset of World War II. We could almost feel how a smoldering turf fire might have taken some of the bite out of countless long nights and days on duty; they used donkeys to bring the turf up.

Martin O'Malley had run up this same hill to ring up Clifden when the Americans had washed ashore. The only telephone in Ailleabreach was installed by the government here.

Our next stop was to the home of Paud and Patsy Kenneelly. Their warm Irish hospitality was especially welcome. Paud, a retired schoolteacher and lifelong resident of Ailleabreach, had been at St. Mary's College in Galway in 1944 and had no first-hand experience with the *Damnyankee* incident. Nevertheless, he was a master at relaying local color, including other stories about bodies washing ashore during the war. One, with a medal on his breast, was identified as a Brit. Another, a German, was buried in the old Church of Ireland cemetery in Ballyconneely after the local village folk decided he was a Lutheran.

It was Paud who told us about the bleak existence of the locals in the West of Ireland during the war years. They struggled for survival with almost no tea, very little bread, living on potatoes.

Michael Conneely, the fisherman with the pitchfork, gave the *Damnyankee* survivors basically everything he had in his effort that day to warm them and reduce their suffering.

Paud also said that for a number of years following the rescue, Trudeau and Vigeant repaid Conneely's kindness by sending him tea, brandy and clothing to say thanks.

We then visited with Josie McNamara, who had been but seven years old in 1944, when the news of the survivors from the sea had spread like wildfire around the little hamlet. Josie had been fascinated, as most kids would be, by the corpse of Henry Beckwith.

"I went down to the beach to see what was going on, before noon, and wasn't there 40 to 50 people standing around the life raft? You know, we saw him lying there, on the beach, and of course it was the first dead person any of us lads had ever seen, with the exception of some old folks, already in the casket, they were.

"This was a bit more exciting now, wasn't it? There was a guard there with him, and didn't he shift us off now? He didn't want us kids hangin' around, causing trouble. It was a beautiful day now, a 'pet' kind of day, a nice day, sandwiched between two bad ones. That often happens right following a storm. I never saw the men again."

We also spoke to Jimmy O'Malley, the fellow who brought whiskey to aid the survivors. Jimmy insisted it was brandy, not whiskey, and that he'd bought it at O'Flaherty's in Ballyconneely, just two days earlier, as he'd the need to fight a bad cold.

Jimmy had lived in England since 1946, returning to Ireland just the year before.

He had been invited to return to Ailleabreach for the monument dedication in 1994, but hadn't the price of the fare. Both Sean and Jim were distressed upon later hearing this from me, as they most certainly would have made the proper arrangements, had they but known. Jimmy remembered the *Damnyankee* survivors well.

"They…those men…were lucky in a way. Had they missed that point in their raft, they'd have been swept into the English Channel, they would, and they'd meet no land."

Like Paud, he had stories about other experiences with military people washing up on the Irish Coast.

"Another time, during the war years, a lifeboat full of sailors, there had to be 20 of them, also washed up, and landed on the strand back there, before these fellas ever came. At least one of them died in the Clifden hospital."

Jimmy wanted to send just one message to Jim Trudeau.

"Well, tell him… tell Jim Trudeau that I hope he lives to be 100."

Our final stop that day was at the little cottage once again, now owned by Gabriel McNamara, the son of Paddy. The place shone like a new copper penny, and we were once again warmly met with a roaring fire, fresh flowers, scones and tea.

What hospitality! I felt such appreciation for the effort made by these wonderful people, to relate their stories and to welcome us. I could only imagine the emotions that must have coursed through Jim Trudeau, when he stood on the same spot at the dedication of the monument.

It had been a vastly entertaining and useful day in Ailleabreach, thanks to Sean's incredible preparation and scheduling.

We returned to Ireland in spring, 2004, going to Olive's now-abandoned home, the original home of the Gavin's, and Clifden Cottage Hospital.

I have made every effort to tell the story of the *Damnyankee* crew in as accurate a manner as I could. With only two survivors alive at the time of this writing, and a time span of six decades, I am confident any mistakes made are the results of memories altered by time, and nothing more.

Following the return to the United States, the crew of the *Damnyankee* went their separate ways, as the war continued to run its course. Despite repeated efforts to track them down, I found little information about the others.

This story is but one of literally thousands that could be told about those who participated in World War II. If my re-telling it helps us to understand and to realize in any way what they dealt with, my work is more than worth the effort.

---Tom Walsh, Driggs, Idaho

ADDENDUM

Notes pertaining to Chapter X: Trouble in the Air

In regards to the final moments of the ditching procedure with the *Damnyankee,* here is an excerpt from a letter Trudeau wrote eight years later, on September 26, 1952. The letter was to Paul H. Nesbitt, Chief of the Arctic, Desert, Tropic Information Center of the Research Studies Institute at Maxwell Air Force Base in Alabama:

"Just before we hit, I rang the alarm. I never heard that bell. There was an ear-splitting racket as the tail of the fuselage smacked the top of a wave, then a grinding, grating, thunderous crash when the nose hit one of those mountains of sea full force. The whole cockpit seemed to explode. Abruptly the tumult ended and there was nothing but the gurgle of water. It had been like riding an eggshell into a concrete wall, then dropping to earth, a sodden mass of waste."

In regards to where the plane crashed: Later estimates have put the location of the ditched PB4Y-1 about six miles west of Inishkea North and Inishkea South Islands, west of the Mullet peninsula and north of Achill Island, off County Mayo in the Irish Republic.

Notes pertaining to Chapter XII: Adrift in the North Atlantic

Trudeau told the Research Studies Institute at Maxwell Air Force Base, "We were too cold to remove our clothing for the purpose of making a sail, and instead used a waterproof chart. It was tiring to hold the chart aloft, spread between two men in the bow, and the pain was excruciating."

Regarding whistling for attention: Eddie Vigeant reported later that, "The next day I learned that a patrolman along the beach had heard my whistle from a distance of about six miles by water and 11 miles by land. The strong wind blowing toward him had helped and yet it was impossible that any of us could have mustered enough strength to make ourselves heard more than a few feet." I was unable to find any further substantiation of this. This, of course, does not mean it didn't happen.

Regarding the crew's overall physical condition: Twelve years later Trudeau told Dr. George Llano, Research and Editorial Specialist at Maxwell Air Force Base's Research Studies Institute; "With the exception of Vigeant, we became physically weak with surprising speed. I attribute much of this to the fact that we had spent several sleepless nights at Goose Bay, in which time we had been briefed repeatedly, at all times of the day or night for flights which subsequently weathered out. Also, we had been under a mental strain for a considerable time prior to the actual ditching, and few of us ate a meal of any consequence. Forced eating might have been good insurance, whether or not we anticipated ditching. Our strength was pretty near gone after 24 hours and it took us one hour to bail six inches of water out of the raft with our shoes."

Notes pertaining to Chapter XIII: Landfall in the West of Ireland

Sean Kelly provided me with a copy of the Irish Army receipt, dated January 16th, 1945, paying 14 shillings to Jimmy O'Malley for the small bottle of whiskey, and fifteen shillings to Michael Conneely for the lost boot. The cost of a live-in farmhand in those days, was perhaps ten shillings a month, plus room and board.

Both Donaldson and Sullivan from the WRGI thought the Irish Army might well have been attempting to ease the suffering of the villagers a bit, as the compensation paid appeared to be quite generous. Times were very difficult in the West of Ireland in the war years.

Notes pertaining to Chapter XIV: Ashore at Ailleabreach

Martin O'Malley's younger brother Jimmy, who was twenty-two, at the advice of his Mum, brought a half-pint of whiskey over to Conneely's house, with the thought it might help to warm the two aviators. Trudeau couldn't even think of it, with his stomach problems, and Vigeant bravely took a swig, but it came back up faster than it went down. Jimmy O'Malley told me, "As things would have it a bit later, the villagers encountered no problems in finishing the rest of the whiskey."

Notes pertaining to Chapter XVII: Leaving Clifden, but for where?

Unbeknownst to the crewmembers, they were headed towards the border of Northern Ireland, which had been a separate state from the

Irish Republic since 1921, following the Irish war for independence from the British.

While the crew of the *Damnyankee* was never advised of either their destination or route taken, the little convoy wound itself northeast along the narrow Connemara roads through Leenane, Westport, and Castlebar, following the same route their departed mate Henry Beckwith had taken a few days earlier.

Notes pertaining to Chapter XVIII: Behind the scenes

Henry Beckwith was interred on foreign soil at Lisnabreeny Cemetery on the outskirts of Belfast. In 1949, his body was exhumed and shipped back to its final resting place, in a military cemetery on New York's Long Island.

Notes pertaining to Chapter XXII: Trudeau returns home

Regarding Admiral Hall: This prestigious leader commanded the 11th Amphibious Force at Omaha Beach on D-Day, as well as the amphibious landings on Sicily at Salerno. A month after meeting Trudeau, he assumed command of the Pacific Fleet Amphibious Force, and directed the amphibious landings at Okinawa in April of 1945.

Dwight David Eisenhower dubbed Hall "the Viking of Assault." To this day, Jim Trudeau has kept his "short snorter" as a memoir of his flight home with the famous Admiral.

Regarding Major Howard: Years later Trudeau found himself reading a magazine article about a multiple murder in the Caribbean. A charter boat captain had apparently gone berserk, and ended up killing not only all of his passengers, but his wife as well. Trudeau's blood ran cold when he saw the photos accompanying the article. The deranged charter skipper appeared to be the former Army Air Corps Major Howard, the very man who he had spent the afternoon talking with more than a decade earlier.

Trudeau told me he felt he must have been right all those years ago, when he first pondered the sanity of a man who would intentionally crash as savage a beast as a B-24, and would do it not just once, but twice.

Notes regarding the Research of this story

Jimmy O'Malley was in poor physical shape when I met with him. He was missing a leg, and had very poor hearing. He was living in a caravan next to his nephew Michael. Jimmy told me, "My nephew doesn't want me to go hungry. They want me to have food all the time. They bring me a meal every day. I can make my own tea in the morning." I thought Jimmy O'Malley was a prince of a man.

Printed in the United States
154403LV00002B/3/P